MODERN MERCHANT BANKING

CLAY AND WHEBLE'S

MODERN
MERCHANT BANKING

⊷

THIRD EDITION

EDITED BY

WILLIAM KAY

WOODHEAD-FAULKNER

NEW YORK LONDON TORONTO SYDNEY TOKYO

Published by Woodhead-Faulkner Limited,
Simon & Schuster International Group,
Fitzwilliam House, 32 Trumpington Street,
Cambridge CB2 1QY, England

First published 1976
Second edition 1983
Third edition 1990

British Library Cataloguing in Publication Data
Clay and Wheble's Modern Merchant Banking. – 3rd ed.
1. London, (City) Merchant banking
I. Clay, C. J. J. (Charles John Jervis)   II. Wheble, B. S.
(Bernard Spenser, *1904*–)   III. Kay, William
332.66′09421′2

ISBN 0-85941-602-X

Designed by Geoff Green
Typeset by Hands Fotoset, Leicester
Printed in Great Britain by BPCC Wheatons Ltd, Exeter

~

CONTENTS

v

PREFACE

SIR MARTIN JACOMB

For many years, since it first appeared, *Modern Merchant Banking* has been the definitive work for those seeking to peer through the mists which have often surrounded the merchant banks of London. The world in which these important businesses operate has become vastly more complex in recent years, and a new edition of the book is thus overdue. I commend this latest version to all who wish to discover more about the varied businesses and services of these resilient houses bearing City names both old and not so old.

PART ONE

SCOPE AND DEVELOPMENT
OF MERCHANT BANKING

1

❧

INTRODUCTION

DEREK HIGGS AND NICHOLAS VEREY

In geographical terms, the City of London is restricted to the north bank of the River Thames and is bounded to the east by Aldgate and Bishopsgate (but including the westernmost warehousing area); to the north by Aldersgate and Moorgate and to the west (nowadays) by a roughly north–south line incorporating the Law Courts, Fleet Street and Hatton Garden – but formerly by Ludgate. In civic terms the City is represented by the Lord Mayor and Commonalty of the City of London. Metaphorically, however, 'The City' has become synonymous with the conglomerate of institutions which comprise the financial centre in which they operate. Headed by the Bank of England, they are the accepting houses; the clearing banks; the discount houses; the other banks (home and overseas); the issuing houses; the investment trusts; The International Stock Exchange; the unit trusts; the Corporation of Lloyd's; the insurance companies; the shipping and commodity exchanges and the London International Financial Futures Exchange and other futures exchanges. It is not the purpose of this book to attempt to define the operations of any of these principal participants other than the accepting houses.

But before doing that, a few paragraphs describing the origins of the City of London and its banking institutions will perhaps help the reader to acclimatise and orientate himself.

Some researchers believe that Celtic Britain boasted a small fortress – with a name that may have sounded like *Lyn-din* – on a northern tributary of the Thames later called the Wall brook. Other historians consider that, having regard to the oak forests and thick scrub which covered the area, anything larger than small farming communities would have been unlikely, if not impossible.

Of course the level of the land on which London now stands is very much higher than it was in the first century – rebuilding and the infilling of low-lying areas has seen to that – but another factor has changed the situation of London and has made archaeological studies somewhat haphazard. The whole of south-eastern England has sunk so as to result in the tidal length of the Thames being greatly increased: in fact, the high-water level is now some 12 to 14 feet above its level in the first century.

3

So, in those early days, the Thames to the west of the Wall brook was certainly shallow enough, at low water, to be forded by the Romans when they invaded from the south and reached the Thames in or around AD 43. The area of the Wall brook found favour with them and they built Londinium there and used it not only as a point of entry for their supplies by sea, but also for the exports of the indigenous products of England, in particular lead, wool, skins and cloth.

Within 300 years Londinium had become one of the most important cities of the Roman Empire and was enclosed by a great stone wall, large sections of which can still be seen both above and below ground. But as the Roman Empire decayed so did the trading station of Londinium, which became virtually deserted by the Romans by the middle of the fifth century.

Of the years after the Roman occupation of Britain, through the Saxon era and until the Norman period there is not much historical record of the life and business of the City of London but, by the time of the arrival of William the Conqueror in the eleventh century, a new township was springing up within the old walls, and trade was being redeveloped with Europe and the East. London was becoming a city of merchants, as it was before and has effectively remained ever since; and we are constantly reminded of that as, in this generation, we move around the City – the names of the streets still reflecting the flourishing markets (or 'cheaps') of those days, for example Eastcheap, Cheapside, Bread Street, Milk Street, Fish Street Hill, Cornhill, Lime Street and many others.

William the Conqueror borrowed heavily from the Jewish community – which had, as the money-lenders of Europe, developed a settlement in London (streets such as Jewry Street and Old Jewry in the City doubtless being named after them) – and began a vast building programme of cathedrals and castles, some of which give the sightseer pleasure today as permanent memorials of the Norman era.

During the late thirteenth century, after a period of persecution, the Jews were largely banished from England and replaced by the Italian bankers, the Lombards, who arrived from Genoa, Venice and Florence, and who became London's principal money-lenders and bankers, giving their name to Lombard Street and laying the foundations for much of our present banking system.

A few centuries later, rudimentary banking experienced a further development through the goldsmiths, who set up shop in Cheapside: they bought bullion, both for their own account and for customers, and issued 'notes' in respect of it, the right to the bullion passing with the 'note' as it changed hands. But banking as we know it today, the taking of deposits and the making of advances, only emerged after Charles I, failing to get the grants of finance he needed from Parliament, sequestrated some £200,000 of the City merchants' money which was lodged with the Royal Mint, then housed in the Tower of London – and after Charles II borrowed £1.3 million from the

Exchequer to fight the War of the Grand Alliance, upon which interest payments were, incidentally, not made for 18 years, leaving the bankers the poorer both in capital and in income. As a clear result of these events, the Bank of England was founded in 1694 under a Royal Charter from William and Mary, in return for a loan of £1.2 million made to the Crown. It was formed, following pleas from the City merchants, to limit and regularise the imposts made by the Crown on the community and, among other business, to maintain the accounts of the merchants and to act as custodians of their growing wealth.

The Bank of England was one of the earliest central banks to be formed in the world – the Bank of Amsterdam in Holland was the first – but it only subsequently developed its role as banker to the Government, note-issuer and lender of last resort to the banking sector, thus to become an important element in the negotiation of bills of exchange, accepted by the accepting houses, to which we later refer.

One more transformation of the City needs to be mentioned since it put an indelible stamp on procedures even as they are today. Towards the end of the seventeenth century, the East India Company started to import coffee into the country and coffee drinking became the fashion. As a result, numerous coffee houses started up in the City – and they became the meeting places for men of the City. There they traded in a variety of commodities and services and, for example, in the house of one, Lloyd, insurances of marine risks were transacted – the precursor of Lloyd's of London, now in Lime Street – and, in the house of another, shares were exchanged and thus The Stock Exchange was born. The messengers of Lloyd's of London and of The Stock Exchange are, to this day, called 'waiters' to remind us of the usage made of the coffee houses and their staff.

It was not until the middle of the eighteenth century that the old City walls were largely pulled down and the City gates removed; but the removal of those restrictive barriers has not, in fact, resulted in much of an 'outflow' of traditional 'City' business to new sites.

So we come to the nineteenth and twentieth centuries in which the accepting houses started to operate in the City, and elsewhere, and gradually – in some cases rapidly – grew to their present eminence in the world of banking.

More recently, however, the accepting houses have met with increasing competition from the joint-stock or 'clearing' banks and this chapter would be incomplete without a brief mention of their development. They are so named because of their common clearing system for the transfer of credit.

From the seventeenth century onwards most main towns in the United Kingdom had at least one private bank, and sometimes more, usually owned and managed by families, which served the domestic banking requirements of individuals and merchants in the area. Clearly, in conditions of slow and inefficient means of communication and travel, those banking relationships were adequate; but as travel became easier and the movement of people and of goods around the country became an everyday matter, a need for a broader-based, intercommunicating, banking system arose. To meet this requirement, a number of leading private banks began to operate together on a wider basis. That development led, in the nineteenth century, to the absorption of most of the country banking system by the bigger London and provincial banks, which itself led to further mergers and aggregations to achieve economies of size and more complete coverage of the whole country. The five remaining English clearing banks and their affiliates in Scotland and Northern Ireland now wield considerable influence but only in comparatively recent times have they developed overseas links and set up subsidiary banking activities in an endeavour to attract the type of business historically carried out by the accepting houses. Indeed each of the major clearing banks now has its merchant banking subsidiary, although the effect of operating under the umbrella of a powerful clearing house parent and the differing histories of most of these subsidiaries have tended to produce a type of merchant bank somewhat different from the rest of the accepting houses.

In addition to the competition between domestic UK banks, there are, as well as the consortium banks, some 257 overseas banks represented in London through branches or subsidiaries which compete for the available banking business. The Bank of England applies an 'open door' policy to the establishment of foreign banks in England, and its flexible approach and the attractions of London as a financial centre have brought to London, especially since 1968, an inflow of foreign banks which compete with the merchant banks in all their fields of business.

While the Bank of England has continued to apply its customary standard of supervision, merchant banks have in recent years come under the additional wing of the Securities and Investments Board. This body was set up under the Financial Services Act 1986, to supervise all companies involved in investment business, acting through a number of self-regulatory bodies covering different aspects of that activity. Merchant banks have always been involved in investment on behalf of clients, but securities-related business has been intensified by the opportunities arising out of the deregulation in 1986 of what is now The International Stock Exchange. This was the series of reforms known colloquially as Big Bang.

The reforms had three main elements. The fixed tariff of minimum commission rates was abolished. So, too, was the rigid distinction between those who dealt in securities as principals – then 'jobbers', now 'market-makers' – and those who acted as brokers on behalf of clients. Finally, companies outside The Stock Exchange were allowed to enter the market as corporate members, and to acquire existing member firms. Previously only individuals could be members of The Stock Exchange, and they could then form themselves into partnerships or, latterly, limited companies.

This last change opened up the London stock market to many other financial organisations, including merchant banks and those clearing banks which had bought merchant banks. Although the enormous ramifications of this development are examined in a later chapter, it is worth noting that as a result the Accepting Houses Committee and the Issuing Houses Association were brought together under the new name of the British Merchant Banking and Securities Houses Association, or BMBA. The new style reflects the diversity of the modern merchant bank, which can be a fund manager, investment adviser, broker, jobber and bank rolled into one. While these functions must be kept distinct, they represent an array of options and challenges unknown to earlier generations. The opportunity for those contemplating a career in merchant banking is unparalleled in living memory.

2

⚮

THE MERCHANT BANKS:
A PROBLEM OF DEFINITION

WILLIAM KAY

Humpty Dumpty in *Alice through the Looking Glass*, when asked by Alice how he could say that the word 'glory' meant a 'nice knockdown argument', said 'It means just what I choose it to mean!' Those who have spent their working lives in merchant banking have no need to imitate Humpty Dumpty: they know what 'merchant banking' means and who the genuine 'merchant bankers' are. They do not follow the path trodden by some financial scribes and politicians in recent years who, although they may have glimpsed the truth, have deliberately by-passed it and, in the way of Humpty Dumpty, have chosen to use the words to mean anything – even if a little unsavoury – that they wished to make them mean. In so doing they have confused the traditional, old-established houses – those that have been described as the Davids of the City, in the sense that their capital and resources are small in comparison with those of the big commercial banks, but who exercise a Goliath's strength and wield a surprising influence – with the new kind of so-called merchant banks which fattened through the lush years of excessive money supply, only to starve, and in some cases die, in the leaner months that followed.

Although much has been written about the City of London itself, there remains great ignorance of its activities and, regrettably, some mistrust of its purpose and methods in the performance of its function as the heart of the financial bloodstream of the country. It would be foolish to pretend that sharp practice could not be found within the so-called square mile, but it is right to say that those institutions which operate in the centre of its financial sector, among which are numbered the accepting houses, have always maintained (and at all times will have to maintain) a strict code of business ethics and morality – otherwise they could not succeed in a nationally and internationally competitive environment in which 'my word is my bond' is the behavioural keynote. This point will be re-emphasised in later chapters and is especially true for the accepting houses for reasons that will be explained.

An Attempted Definition of Merchant Banking

Merchant banks in London, at least those that will still answer to the term, are

8

now seldom merchants and by no means always bankers. The phrase is often purloined as a generic description of businesses that operate in the financial sector, whether or not they perform pure banking or merchanting services.

In the past there was nothing to prevent any business erecting a brass plaque on its premises and describing itself as a 'merchant bank'. However, since the passing of the Banking Act 1979, no person may describe his business as a bank or himself as a banker unless the Bank of England says so. This authorisation was amended by the Banking Act 1987, which insists that an institution has to fulfil minimum criteria before the Bank will authorise it, mainly to do with conducting business prudently, and with integrity and skill. The directors, controllers and managers must be fit and proper, and the bank has to have net assets of at least £1 million. Of course, having obtained such authorisation as a *bank*, it is entirely a matter for the shareholders whether it should call itself a *merchant bank*, or for that matter an investment bank or even a securities house.

The main difficulty in trying to establish a clear definition of what constitutes a merchant bank is that the sector has been under constant change, especially during the 1980s. Deregulation and globalisation have pushed and pulled and tugged at the relevant companies and those in their immediate vicinity, and the debate is overlaid with international variations. The French banque d'affaires and the American investment bank are recognisably cousins of the merchant bank as it is to be encountered in London today.

This maelstrom of change was formally recognised in 1988, when the hallowed Accepting Houses Committee and its junior counterpart, the Issuing Houses Association, were replaced by the British Merchant Banking and Securities Houses Association, a list of whose members are listed in Appendix A. Its first annual report declared:

The BMBA has been created to fulfill the functions of a trade association for firms active in the merchant banking and securities industry. The principal purpose of the Association is to represent the interests of its members in relation to any aspect of their business and to lobby or negotiate on their behalf with the various authorities in the United Kingdom, the European Community or elsewhere.

The BMBA's scope can be judged by the names of its committees. There are four Functional Committees: Asset Management, Compliance, Corporate Finance and Securities Trading. Another nine Specialist Committees cover areas of particular interest: Administration/Premises, Accountants, Economists Group, Export Finance, Internal Audit, Personnel, Securities Managers, Taxation, VAT Practitioners. All these Specialist Committees existed under the aegis of the Accepting Houses Committee and have simply continued their work on behalf of their new parent.

The activities of merchant banks were originally, and still are, intimately connected with foreign trade and with the international movement of goods and services. But the nature of their business has changed. Once it was that of the merchant venturer and, therefore, concerned primarily with merchanting for their own account. The term 'accepting house' arose from the service of accepting – i.e. giving cash in advance for – companies' bills of exchange to provide short-term finance. That function involved fine judgements as to the creditworthiness of the company in question, bringing the accepting house into a close relationship with its clients.

However, modern bank customers have a complex of interrelated problems and requirements, to each of which there may be a number of possible and entirely feasible answers. Indeed, banks of all kinds compete vigorously with one another to offer new services, to meet an ever wider range of possible requirements.

All that unites them is that they all serve primarily, though not exclusively, the corporate sector. In doing so they provide financial advice as to the most appropriate steps for their clients to take to safeguard or enhance their interests. That advice may require the execution of skills in banking, mergers and acquisitions, stockbroking, money-broking, market-making, investment management, bullion dealing or anything else which falls within the law. Such skills may be executed by the merchant bank, but not necessarily. The City of London is amply populated with sufficient specialists to carry out any of these requirements, although no merchant bank worthy of the name is likely to subcontract the banking and corporate finance functions. More importantly, the modern corporate client is liable to want those skills to be available in every major financial centre, suitably adapted to conform with local custom and practice. It is the modern merchant bank's task to ensure that it can execute its clients' every need in every corner of the globe.

3

❧

THE MERCHANT VENTURER

WILLIAM KAY

The concept of the merchant venturer was the starting-point for many of the accepting houses. Some, it is true, had their beginnings as a result of more positive leanings towards banking and finance, but all were established or eventually attracted to operate in London, where liberal surroundings beckoned them.

It does not take much imagination to appreciate the problems that the accepting houses met and had to overcome. The past two centuries are packed with factors that formed a backcloth for difficult trading conditions in which only the tenacious and the skilled could survive. To name but a few: revolutions – industrial, commercial, social and political; wars – continental and intercontinental, Napoleonic and others, leading up to the two world wars of our century; recession; and inflation.

The merchant venturer built his success on a number of special characteristics in his make-up. Perhaps the most important were as follows:

1. *Integrity* – a determination to build and then to protect his good name; his determination to ensure that he always lives up to the belief that his word is as good as his bond, not only at home but also abroad, binding him as surely as the most carefully worded and legally executed legal contract.
2. *Expertise* – the intangible, technical skill which derives from a mixture of tradition, experience and, most important of all, dedication, coupled with natural flair to distinguish between the good and the bad in matters of business.
3. *Adaptability and imagination* – which condition a man's flexibility of outlook and approach to change.
4. *Tenacity* – giving no quarter to defeat even in periods of extreme crisis and disaster to others. Certainly there have been defeats and temporary difficulties among the accepting houses, but the debts have been repaid and the businesses rebuilt.

Transition from Merchant Venturer to Accepting House

It is important to recognise how the merchant venturer made use of the qualities named to bring about his transition from being a merchant for his own account to being both that and a banker for merchants.

It has already been mentioned that, in their beginnings, many merchant bankers occupied themselves principally in overseas trade. Some used their own (or chartered) ships to convey manufactured goods from the then developed countries of Europe to, for example, the countries of North and South America and the Far East, where they sold them direct or through local agents, or, later, through their own offices in those countries, which were frequently managed by members of the merchant venturer's own family. With the proceeds, indigenous products were purchased, usually, in fact, in earliest days by direct barter, and shipped back to Europe.

From the beginning, while they were buying, shipping and selling for their own account, merchant bankers developed a network of overseas connections for whom they bought in Europe, subsequently selling products from overseas for account of the same parties.

Their overseas connections became – and often remained – their banking clients, who deposited with them the proceeds of the sale, in Europe, of their local products; thus, too, their overseas customers became investors in the United Kingdom and also invested in bonds and shares of other overseas countries, relying on the merchant bank to care for their investments, to collect their dividends and to finance their shipments, whether of manufactured goods inwards or indigenous raw materials outwards. Finance for shipments from the overseas country was usually arranged by the exporter drawing a bill of exchange on his merchant bank for an agreed proportion of the value of the cargo and by selling that bill of exchange (the bill on London) to a local banker at a discount. The local banker then forwarded the bill to his London agent who presented it, accompanied by the shipping documents, to the merchant banker, who would 'accept' it as duly payable on a date stated and retain the shipping documents. The due date for payment of the bill – previously agreed with the shipper – would be decided upon to allow for the goods to be sold and the payment to be received before the merchant bank was required to pay the value of the bill. Thus the shipper received the main value for his shipment when the ship was loaded; the intermediate banker received interest, by way of discount on his purchase price for the bill in the first place, for the money he advanced; and the merchant banker charged his overseas client an acceptance commission for the privilege given to the client by way of an undertaking to accept the bill on first presentation in London.

It was in this way the accepting houses built up their original overseas banking connections and also the way in which they built up their reputation for fair and honest dealing.

Of course, so long as the values of the goods purchased and sold were in balance, no need for international transfers of funds existed, but the merchant bankers tended, later, to alter the pattern of their business to such an extent that their exports and imports were brought into a state of imbalance, thus creating a need for international movements of credit; and so, as business developed, London became the centre of world trade and sterling the world's trading currency – even for goods that, in fact, never touched England's shores. This development led to a special use of the bill of exchange, whereby credit was transferred from one overseas country to another by means of a bill drawn in sterling on a London banker, the bill being saleable by the beneficiary either to a local banker or, less expensively, to another local merchant who was buying goods in London and needed the sterling to pay for them.

Use of the bill of exchange was later recognised and expressed in the Bills of Exchange Act 1882 in the following words:

A Bill of Exchange is an unconditional order in writing, addressed by one person to another, signed by the person giving it, requiring the person to whom it is addressed to pay on demand or at a fixed or determinable future time a sum certain in money to or to the order of a specified person or to bearer.

But, of course, even the legal definition, when introduced, was of no value to the owner of the bill unless he could absolutely rely upon the drawee to pay on the agreed date. Many London merchants did possess good reputations and bills were freely and fearlessly drawn on them; but there were evident dangers to the holders of a bill drawn on a less creditworthy name and so the habit grew up of 'borrowing' the name of a fully trusted London merchant and paying the latter a commission for his acceptance and due payment of the bill – thus the title 'accepting house'.

Further Sophistication in the Use of the Sterling Bill of Exchange

So these international merchant bankers – the accepting houses of today – began their gradual change into bankers for international merchants, as well as for international trade, and enlarged their spheres of operation and of influence by accepting bills of exchange drawn on them by the sellers of goods of which they might not themselves be the purchasers – bills of exchange drawn to finance international trading transactions to which they themselves were not necessarily a party.

In the nineteenth century, the bill on London, which was the very essence of the accepting house, became the main instrument of payment for all goods and produce moving internationally. A bill drawn on one of the accepting houses, under authority of a letter of credit issued to the drawer by the accepting house, was not only the preferred means of international payment but also frequently preferable to local currency, although the bill itself was almost invariably expressed in sterling – settlements between Philadelphia and Boston, for example, until well after the Civil War, were most easily carried out by sterling bills on London.

With a merchant's understanding of mercantile problems, the accepting houses made this business simple for a seller of goods, and for the buyer, by creating a variation of the letter of credit (in fact, an old banking instrument which, in its simple form, was used by the Greeks way back in the fourth century BC. For their special purpose the nineteenth-century merchant bankers called it a documentary letter of credit (now simply called a 'documentary credit') and introduced a condition into it. At the request of the actual buyer of the goods, and in accordance with his detailed instructions, they authorised the seller to draw his bill of exchange on them and undertook to accept it on first presentation *provided that* it was accompanied by specified shipping and other documents relating to the goods. The seller could be perfectly sure that he would be drawing a bill of exchange which was 'as safe as the Bank of England' and that, as a result, he could at once sell it to someone else and thus receive its present value in hard cash immediately. The buyer could still get his period of credit, making his own arrangements with the merchant banker regarding release of the goods, either on providing funds in cover or in anticipation of so doing. The merchant banker, charging a commission for this use of his name, had to meet the accepted bill of exchange at maturity for the honour of that name even if the buyer had failed to carry out his part of the bargain, i.e. to provide funds in cover at the latest at the date of maturity.

Thus, knowledge, tradition, the good name of specialist houses and the international information to which they had access via agents or correspondents overseas were used to extend credit facilities to people in all parts of the world.

4

≈

THE NEXT PHASE: SPECIALISATION

WILLIAM KAY

Overseas Loans

Arising out of their overseas connections thus developed, the accepting houses grew to be recognised as bankers, and as consultants on banking and investment matters, not only by their UK and overseas private customers, but also by overseas local and central governments. They were recognised as having special knowledge of the areas in which they operated, and London became the principal financial centre where overseas borrowers could raise loans by bond issues. Hence, as many 'underdeveloped' overseas countries began their long trek towards 'development', their local and central governments came to take financial advice from the London accepting houses and to raise loans in Europe and elsewhere, employing the accepting houses, as their agents, to issue the loans and to service them on their behalf.

The zenith of the political influence of the accepting houses was probably reached during the Napoleonic Wars and the two decades which followed, when the foreign policies of the Great Powers depended heavily on the international financial arrangements which only the merchant bankers could provide. But simultaneously with these operations and subsequently up until 1914 the accepting houses, through the raising of loans, financed the infrastructure required to market world-wide the manufactured goods which were emerging from the Industrial Revolution on the one hand and, on the other hand, the purchase of food and raw materials which were increasingly being produced in faraway lands to meet the demands of the industrial countries.

The canal age was being supplanted by the railway, the clipper ship by the steamship. Both in the United States and in Canada, railways which linked Atlantic to Pacific, the Trans-Siberian Railway in Asia, the railways of Europe, South America and the Indian sub-continent, all looked to the accepting houses for finance. Waterworks, docks and other public works of every kind around the world were financed by loans, raised on the London market, of funds subscribed predominantly by the increasingly rich British merchants and manufacturers, but in large part, too, from foreign investors who regarded sterling as the most trustworthy currency for investment.

So it was that an international market in international loans grew up in the City of London, only to be crippled by the aftermath of war and resulting exchange control. In the meantime, however, many trading benefits accrued to the UK banking and industrial sectors from the initiative displayed in these matters by the accepting houses – some of which also took a principal role in underwriting and marketing British Government debt, prior to the appointment of the Bank of England to perform that function.

Sterling as a World Currency

As an adjunct to their paramount position in the overseas banking field, the accepting houses held deposits not only for their overseas customers and associates but also for foreign governments. Thus the growth of the accepting houses was inextricably interwoven into the history of sterling as a world currency and this factor, together with the growth of the financial reserves of Britain's colonial empire which were deposited in London, and with the financial reserves of many other countries who chose, as the highest-degree security, to hold their reserves in sterling, provided London with the then unchallengeable role of provider of world-wide development finance and the currency in which virtually all international indebtedness was settled.

Simultaneously with their development of business in bills of exchange, the accepting houses became the central market for that type of financial instrument, which itself became accepted as a form of international currency. Indeed, such was the predominance of sterling as a currency, in the form of bills on London, for the settlement of international indebtedness, that on the outbreak of the First World War in 1914, when bank rate was raised to 10%, the American money market, together with other financial markets around the world, was thrown into a state of near collapse.

Domestic Activities

Short-term Lending: Acceptance Credits

In 1931 the Macmillan Committee reported as follows:

In connection with short-term credit, all concerned would benefit by a more extended use of commercial bills.

This led to the adaptation by the accepting houses of their acceptance facilities so as to result in their greater use by the home trade (in the form of acceptance credits) to finance short-term requirements such as, for example, the financing of raw materials in bonded warehouses pending processing, manufacture and sale. With interest rates low and an adequate supply of money in the discount market for the purchase of bills of exchange, it often proves cheaper for industry to borrow on a short-term basis in this way, extending the borrowing at maturity by drawing a 'renewal' bill of exchange, the discount of which provides funds to meet the maturing one.

It must be appreciated and emphasised, however, that the purposes for which it was, and still is, permissible to use acceptance credits are more restricted than those applying to bank overdrafts. A bill of exchange, to be acceptable for rediscount by the Bank of England as the lender of last resort to the banking sector, must be related to a self-liquidating current transaction that will be completed within the term ('tenor') of the bill – and that should not normally exceed three to four months. Furthermore, bill finance can be appropriate for short-term borrowing only if both the drawer and the acceptor are satisfied that a ready market exists for the bill in the money-market within the City of London; and that the discount market, which is normally the first buyer, will buy the bill at the finest discount rate because it can, if necessary, tender it to the Banker of England as first-class security for its own required borrowings from the central bank.

Of course, the accepting house must pay the bill at maturity, whether or not cash cover has been provided to it by its customer. However inconceivable, it is worth saying that the money-market system in the City would be thrown into confusion if an accepting house failed to honour its own acceptance at maturity – and that has never happened.

Other Short- to Medium-term Lending

The accepting houses do not benefit from the great volume of interest-free current accounts which are principally held by the clearing banks, largely from their private banking clients. The accepting houses do, none the less, make short-term direct loan facilities available to their customers on terms that compare with those offered by the clearing banks and they finance these by 'buying' deposits from their customers and other banks – whether in sterling or in foreign currencies.

Thus, it may be claimed that the accepting houses compete directly with other banks in the provision of loan facilities and so offer to their clients alternative sources of short-term finance – fixed advance or acceptance credit – which can be used according to which is the cheaper and/or more appropriate for the particular transaction. The versatility of the accepting houses in these fields is unmatched.

At the longer end of their short- to medium-term lending activities, the accepting houses were largely instrumental in developing the provision of finance for high-value export contracts based upon a guarantee of the overseas buyer granted by the Export Credits Guarantee Department of the Secretary of State for Trade (ECGD). Some years ago, operating overseas in a manner similar to that of their ancestors, the accepting houses reinforced their studies of the requirements of overseas buyers for UK manufactured goods and jointly with the manufacturers themselves, and supported by the ECGD, fostered a high percentage of UK exports on credit terms. In later times other agencies, particularly the clearing banks, have played an increasing part in this type of business, but the accepting houses are still leading the field in arranging large export contracts for UK suppliers, thus again showing their adaptability and imagination in business development.

Corporate Finance

Before the Second World War the accepting houses acted as issuers of bonds and managers of loans for overseas – and, later, for domestic – borrowers in an important way. After the Second World War they developed their corporate finance capability and have taken the leading role in raising permanent and long-term finance within the United Kingdom and, for UK borrowers, overseas. The increasing need for industry to regroup into larger, more cost-effective units and other financial pressures and distortions brought about the take-over and merger situations of which much has been heard in recent years. The accepting houses, and the other issuing houses, are the leaders in the provision of expert advice to both (or all) parties in these situations, as well as in the field of new issues and other financial transactions where regrouping and reconstruction is necessary to the continued success of the organisation concerned.

International Capital Market

Following on the development of the international money market, an important new international capital market has developed since 1963. Although it has spread during this period right across the world, encompassing the principal European capitals as well as Tokyo, Singapore and other cities, London is still its centre. The accepting houses have made a significant contribution to the pioneering and expansion of this market and numerous British companies and public institutions have had access to it.

Bond issues in the international capital market are made in all the major convertible currencies. The bonds are purchased, for the most part, by investors in countries outside that of the currency in which the loan is denominated. The most important segment of this market has been developed in issues in US dollars, subscribed by non-residents of the United States. Very large amounts have, however, also been raised in Deutschmarks, Dutch guilders, sterling, Swiss, French, Belgian and Luxembourg francs, Japanese yen and certain Arabian currencies, as well as in combinations of currencies such as sterling/Deutschmarks, European Units of Account, European Currency Units and Special Drawing Rights.

In first helping to create these new forms of business, and then in building them up, the accepting houses can claim to have sponsored the development of the new international money market (the Eurocurrency market) and the international capital market (the Eurobond market), to the great advantage of the UK balance of payments, and the financing of world trade.

Investment Advisory Services

The Radcliffe Report said:

Investment Advisory Service is something in which the accepting houses specialise to a far greater extent than other financial institutions ... they manage, or have advisory influence upon the management of, private investments amounting to hundreds of millions of pounds.

This remains true today, although the figures, now thousands of millions of pounds worth, are much higher than in 1959 when the Radcliffe Report was published.

The accepting houses cover the entire sphere of investment advice: they advise private and institutional clients; they manage pension funds, investment trusts and unit trusts. As a separate allied function, they play an important part in the underwriting of new issues.

It is sometimes questioned whether the same house that is advising, for example, an industrial company on reconstruction or on a merger or takeover should be entitled also to be advising clients on investment portfolios which may, fortuitously, include investments in that client company. The Panel on Takeovers and Mergers investigated this subject in depth in 1969–70. This interesting Report is noteworthy for the evaluation it makes of the high standard of integrity maintained by the accepting houses.

5

e~o

MERCHANT BANKING TODAY

DEREK HIGGS AND NICHOLAS VEREY

Merchant banks reflect the character and style of the people who run them. They have always been evolving, although major changes have taken place in response to new operating conditions. For long periods these conditions have been reasonably stable. However, from time to time major external events conspire to make these changes more dramatic and more significant to the outside world.

Major changes occured in the mid 1980s. These are attributed in the minds of many outside observers to the deregulation of the stock-market in 1986, known as Big Bang. But the macroeconomic factors which created the massive changes in the environment in which merchant banks operate had been building for many years. People have different views as to when this process started. For many, one of the factors will be the oil shocks of the early 1970s. The financial surpluses, and subsequent deficits, which the OPEC countries developed were the first of a series of major financial flows across the world's exchanges. The surpluses which resulted from the rise in the price of oil were moved into the world's banking system and then around it.

During the 1970s also, a number of governments set in train initiatives to ease or dismantle exchange controls, and the tax disadvantages of international investment were also reduced. It had become clear that exchange controls did not have the desired effect of reducing capital outflows but, rather, created distortions. In most cases there were ways round them or methods of avoidance which, whilst expensive, remained attractive, especially since it was usually worth paying the necessary premium to invest outside a weakening currency. The incentive to invest outside the stronger currencies was correspondingly less. The 1979 suspension of exchange controls in the United Kingdom did not lead to an immediate outflow of funds, and the extent of overseas investment was no more and no less than expected. The abolition was, however, crucial to the development of London although the biggest capital market of all, the Eurodollar market, has always operated outside exchange controls and national government regulation. The result of dismantling exchange controls was that corporations and institutions were free to move funds across borders and they increasingly took advantage of this freedom over the ensuing years.

At the end of the 1970s the trade fortunes of the United States and Japan changed dramatically. In part to achieve growth, the US government allowed its budget deficit to increase to previously unthought-of levels. The United States also became a major debtor nation. Growth in the US economy and the consequent increase in imports led to a rising trade deficit which was in part also the result of a major increase in the US oil import bill. Mirroring this and partly as a result of it, Japan was achieving a rapidly rising trade surplus. Again, these deficits and surpluses resulted in massive financial flows across exchanges.

The move towards the institutionalisation of markets continued strongly throughout the 1970s. The advantages to the individual of having his savings managed professionally, whether through pension funds, unit trusts or insurance policies, increased. The combination of effective salesmanship and, in some countries, the tax advantages of such saving accelerated this growth. Thus the ownership of companies in Europe, the United States and the Far East was moving inexorably into the hands of the big investing institutions and away from individuals. The concentration of shareholdings in institutional hands led to much larger securities transactions, and therefore a requirement for more capital for securities houses. Privatisation and tax incentives to the individual investor in certain countries slowed this trend, but did not halt it. Thus the percentage of dealings in the world's stock markets by institutions rose strongly throughout this period.

At the same time these institutions, as a result of the pressure put on them for better investment performance, were constantly searching for higher returns or diversification of risk. This led them to look increasingly at investment opportunities in overseas markets. The thrust towards international investment was made either to benefit from more rapid economic growth in other geographic areas, or to achieve the advantages of diversification available through other currencies and economies. In parallel, corporations world-wide became more sophisticated in the management of their treasury operations, and in particular where they maintained their cash balances. The management of cash became an international rather than domestic activity and the hedging of income flows in foreign currencies became a major concern. The growth in hedging instruments such as futures and options and the forward markets bore testimony to this trend.

Thus throughout the world the flow of funds across the various exchanges grew dramatically. This inevitably created pressure on the practitioners, whether they were commercial banks, merchant banks, stockbrokers or foreign exchange traders. For the City of London the increasingly international aspect of these developments meant that in order to maintain their competitiveness, merchant banks had to deal with international products and clients in the face of international competition. Their methods of business, the structure of their ownership and capital adequacy all came into question.

Many participants in the financial services industry world-wide focused their thinking on the events taking place in London, not least because London was the natural centre of a third major financial time zone, the other two being based on New York and Tokyo. In the background, for those prescient enough to see them, 1992 and the coming of the single European internal market were visible on the distant horizon. At the same time, dramatic developments in technology led to rapid improvements in communications and the speed of executing transactions. This led the securities industry to believe that it would be necessary to be able to trade in one centre in each major time zone, further increasing the importance of London.

The larger corporations began looking overseas for further expansion, feeling they were constrained within the United Kingdom. Some merchant banks decided to follow their clients and develop international merger and acquisition capability. The United States was for many companies the most attractive prospect, for political, financial and commercial reasons. But it also possessed the most developed and competitive investment banking industry in the world. So, although the United States was clearly an attractive opportunity for UK merchant banks, it meant competing in the domestic market with the strongest competition. As a result the pressure to expand, diversify and strengthen their capital base became of paramount importance to most merchant banks.

While these major developments were gathering speed, the Office of Fair Trading had referred the London Stock Exchange to the Restrictive Practices Court so that its rule-book could be thoroughly examined. In 1983 the Conservative Government and the London Stock Exchange agreed that if the latter undertook to change a number of its rules, the case before the Restrictive Practices Court would be dropped. This was the agreement which ultimately ushered in Big Bang. Although many rules were involved, those of particular significance concerned fixed minimum commissions, single capacity and outside membership. Up to that time brokers' commissions were not negotiable and the rules precluded brokers from making markets and jobbers from dealing direct with investing clients. This, together with the inability of outsiders to join the Stock Exchange, was considered a restriction on the competition which the Government wished to encourage. While the deregulation which resulted from the agreement was in fact a relatively local development when put in a world context, it set in train new strategic thinking within the City of London and heralded a climate of change.

It was always probable that in London international pressure, even without Big Bang, would lead to considerable changes in the ownership, structure and operations of merchant banks. The securities industry and merchant banks had for many years worked so closely together that major changes in one were likely to influence major changes in the other. In addition, parallel developments could be seen in a number of other important financial services sectors. Insurance companies and building societies wished to broaden the services offered to their customers. The mood was of change and relatively few were prepared to stand aside and miss what appeared to be unrepeatable opportunities for acquisition or new ventures.

In this climate there were broadly three choices for merchant banks: to remain small and specialist, to develop a medium-sized business covering a number of selected areas, or to develop a fully-integrated investment bank with a profile similar to those operating in New York.

The specialists saw the attractions of flexibility, a low-cost base and the advantage of sticking to skills already acquired without the need for increased capital.

Those pursuing the medium-sized strategy felt capable of developing their business without wishing to embark on solving some of the more significant problems involved in creating a completely new and unfamiliar institution. They also found than an alliance of an apparently benign sort provided the capital which they lacked. Many foreign entrants found that this form of access to capital was the most acceptable and risk-free method of entry.

The rationale for the investment bank choice was that, in an increasingly competitive international world, the methods already evolved in the United States and the Euromarkets would soon be replicated in London. In order to compete it would necessary to be structured in a similar way. After all, driving on the left-hand side of the road is all very well in London, but dangerous in Paris or New York. More particularly, the distribution of new securities would be a vital adjunct to the traditional issuing and merger and acquisition business of the merchant banks. In order to build a strong distribution system it would be necessary to have a major presence in the secondary markets involving investment research, sales and trading. It was also argued that there would be opportunities to cross-sell the services of one division to the clients of another, thus increasing profitability.

For many foreign entrants, therefore, the acquisition of a member of The Stock Exchange was either an important part of their global strategy or, at its least, seen as the acquisition of a seat at the table where the most far-reaching changes were taking place in any of the world's securities markets.

Domestically, most participants were concerned about the erosion of their traditional business either from strengthened local competition or the very profitable competitors from overseas, especially the United States and Japan. Clearing banks, worried by the trend towards securitisation of debt and thus the weakening of their lending business, felt it necessary to develop a greater ability to trade all types of securitised instruments. Merchant banks were concerned that the inability to distribute securities would weaken their profitable mergers and acquisition business, so much of which was dependent upon equity finance. But for these companies the strategic decision to trade securities globally was not vindicated in the years immediately following Big Bang, while developments in the market since October 1987 rendered the more modest acquisitions unprofitable and probably irrelevant. As managements review their strategic decisions for the 1990s, it seems probable that a secondary phase of reconstruction of the securities industry in particular and the financial services industry in general may take place.

The costs involved in supplying global services to their clients are a test for the resources and stamina of all but the strongest merchant banks. However, recent developments have been so fundamental that a return to parochialism for merchant banks, or indeed their international competitors, seems unlikely. The challenge will be to adopt the appropriate financial structure and ownership profile and develop businesses profitably at great distances from the home base, whilst at the same time retaining sufficient flexibility to adapt to further changes in the economic and business environment which are inevitable.

PART TWO

PROVISION OF RESOURCES

6

❧

SHORT-TERM FINANCE

CLARK MCGINN

Merchant banks owe their name to their history of providing credit to international traders to enable them to finance their trading shipments. Traditionally, the merchant bank would accept a trader's bill of exchange and then sell that accepted bill (or 'acceptance') into the market specialising in that paper. When the goods were sold the trader would have enough cash to give to the merchant bank to enable the bank to cover the acceptance when presented. This was, therefore, a self-liquidating form of short-term finance.

Obviously the price obtained in the market for that paper was a reflection of the credit-worthiness of the merchant bank and an elite group of banks became the 'accepting houses', those whose names could command the finest pricing. Interestingly, when the gilt-market was being discussed by the Victorian writer Walter Bagehot (1826–77), he said that Government paper should be of such recognised credit that it would be more acceptable than a bill accepted by Barings. Nowadays, facilities are not confined to acceptances but are also available to provide borrowings in cash.

The common feature of these drawings in cash and be acceptances is their short-term nature. A drawing would be allowed for a fixed period of, say, one, three or six months but the bank would retain the right to cancel the facility at any time.

Acceptances

The acceptance credit remains a straightforward method of raising finance, linked to the movement of goods by drawing a bill of exchange on a prime-name bank in the City. These banks are no longer only the traditional merchant banks, but include the clearing banks and major international banks as well. The banks accept the bills for sale to the discount market and some other market-makers at the very fine rates they can command.

Nowadays, the mechanical side remains almost exactly the same as in Victorian times. The customer (who will be a trader in, or manufacturer of, goods approved for this purpose by the Bank of England) will draw a bill on the bank who will accept it (thus taking primary responsibility to pay the bill at maturity). The bill will be for an amount of between £250,000 and £1 million and if a customer seeks to draw a greater sum, a series of bills would be accepted. As this is a short-term financing, bills are drawn to mature after a fixed period usually from one month up to a maximum of 187 days. This is often called the 'usance' of the bill.

Once the bill is accepted the customer will receive the face value of the bill less the discount factor (which is a function of the cost to the discount market of holding the bill to maturity) and the acceptance commission (which is the bank's margin, being a direct function of the bank's analysis of the creditworthiness of the borrower: for top 'blue chip' borrowers this may be in the order of hundreths of 1 percent, for smaller concerns, perhaps 2 or 3 percent).

At maturity of the bill, whoever in the market is holding it will present it to the bank (as acceptor) and will receive the full face value. The customer will have given a formal undertaking (usually in the form of a facility letter between it and the bank) and will remit funds to cover the face value. Often the customer will draw new bills which, when discounted, will generate the funds to cover the maturing bills. This is called 'rolling over'.

Why is such an antiquated system still in use?

The Bank of England uses the commercial bill market to influence short-term rates (leaving market forces to influence longer-term rates). To a lesser degree the Bank of England also deals in Treasury and Local Authority Bills.

The importance of this market is the way in which its operations regulate the net liquidity of the money-market and the flow of funds between the commercial banks and the Bank of England. If a shortage appears likely in the market (which can occur on a daily basis, e.g. by a rise in note circulation, by calls on gilts or when there are large net payments to the Exchequer for tax) the Bank of England, which undertakes to make good any short-term deficiency, will indicate to the discount houses that it is prepared to purchase bankers' acceptances from them. The discount houses respond by offering bills at a price which may or may not be the rate at which the Bank is buying bills in a given maturity. Obviously strong demand for commercial bills by the Bank of England affects the pattern of interest rates subject to the expected availability of short-term funds in the discount market; for the price of bills will tend to rise and, hence, the eligible bill rate will fall compared with other money-market rates.

This was most evident in the period up to November 1985 when the authorities sought to control the persistent rise in UK bank lending (and therefore £M3) by 'overfunding', i.e. by the sale of larger amounts of debt to the non-bank private sector than was needed to fund the Public Sector Borrowing Requirement. The scale of this exercise would have caused significant liquidity problems in the market were it not for the Bank of

England providing relief by continued purchasing of commercial bills. As a result, the Bank of England rapidly accumulated large holdings of these bills – the so-called bill mountain. This tended further to distort the relationship between eligible bill and interbank rates.

Although the policy of 'match funding' was announced in the Mansion House speech in 1985, there are still few signs that the Bank of England is to change its general policy on commercial bills, to remove their pricing advantage altogether.

Cash advances

As there are a number of transactions or industries which cannot be financed by acceptances, there is a significant demand for banks to lend in cash (either in sterling or in foreign currencies). Also, of course, there are occasions when the interest rates applicable to cash drawings are lower than the bill rates. Merchant banks, therefore, either provide facilities with acceptance credit/ cash advance options or straight cash advances.

The methodology is not dissimilar to drawing in bills. A borrower will elect to draw an amount (usually a multiple of £250,000) for a fixed period of up to 12 months, called the interest period.

At the beginning of the interest period the bank will fix an interest rate for that period, in line with the rates which the London market is quoting for deposits in the relevant currency for the amount and period of the cash advance: this rate is called the London Interbank Offered Rate, or LIBOR. At the end of the interest period the borrower will pay the bank the aggregate of the LIBOR and the bank's margin, and has the option either to repay the principal, or roll it over, for a further interest period.

Other lending facilities

Borrowing in cash or bills will cover the bulk of any company's likely requirement. However, banks can offer a range of ancillary facilities to cover more specialised situations. These include providing letters of credit, which are a method of financing international trade, giving security to both vendor and purchaser. Obviously, the vendor is loth to release his goods prior to payment, while the purchaser is equally concerned about paying for a consignment outside his physical control and, perhaps, on another continent. The letter of credit is a compromise whereby a bank promises to make payments to a vendor provided that a series of documents (which might confirm quality, amount, shipment, etc.) are presented to the bank or its overseas correspondents. Upon satisfactory receipt of these papers, the bank makes payment on behalf of the purchaser who will then receive documents giving ownership of the shipment.

Other facilities might be to give guarantees to HM Customs and Excise in respect of VAT payments, or guarantees to professional or regulatory bodies; or in the discounting of a company's debtors, where the bank 'buys' debts due to its customer, releasing cash more quickly than in the normal terms of trade available to the customer.

A merchant bank tries to bring these financing methods together to make a comprehensive set of options for each of its customer's borrowing needs.

7

❧

MEDIUM-TERM FINANCE

CLARK MCGINN

Short-term finance is best suited to meet working capital needs. However, companies also have longer-term requirements, perhaps to finance a major asset purchase, or an acquisition, or to refinance a persistent (or 'hard core') element of short-term debt. In each of these cases, the company would seek to match the medium-term value of its asset with medium-term debt, rather than having an on-demand line which could be called by its bankers at any time.

There are, of course, some features about term-lending on loan account that make it different from lending on a short-term basis. The two main differences are as follows:

1. Once a medium-term loan is agreed, the advance cannot be repaid on demand by the bank as the term of the loan (i.e. the length of time the facility is made available) is agreed at the beginning between bank and borrower and must be adhered to, provided that the borrower does not fall behind with its repayments, or break some other fundamental term or condition of the original offer.
2. Because the bank will be committing its funds to a borrower for a number of years it will often require security, either over the asset itself, over all of the assets of a company ('a debenture') or in the form of guarantees from parent or fellow subsidiary companies. It may wish to insist on building certain written safeguards into the loan agreement (called 'covenants'). For example, these might prevent the customer from becoming over-extended in its borrowing during the course of the loan, or restrict its ability to take up further secured loans from other lenders, or specify the amount of working capital to be kept in the business, or similar criteria.

There are four main factors which can be varied to create a loan suitable to the size and requirement of any given company. They are as follows:

1. The term of the loan.
2. The interest rate charged.
3. The security and covenants given.
4. The fees paid to the bank.

Medium-term lending covers the range from over one year to between five and seven years. Greater than that is specialised long-term finance, although one way to extend medium-term lines is for the bank to grant an 'evergreen' facility. If, for example, the initial term is for three years, after each year, if the borrower's credit warranted it, one further year would be added to the term, restoring it to a three-year facility.

In the case of a loan for asset purchases, the term of the loan is really determined by the expected useful life of the asset. For example, in the case of a loan to purchase leasehold property, the term of the loan would not extend beyond the term of the lease. In any given case, the loan is generally repaid from the benefit obtained from the asset over its useful life or from disposals of surplus, acquired assets or from the general corporate cashflow. There are areas (like hotel financing or management buy-outs) where a proportion of the debt will be repaid over the medium term with a view to refinancing a lower level of debt upon the loan's maturity.

Depending on the type of asset, and the borrower's standing, there are a number of different ways of repaying the loan over the term. The most straightforward is called 'bullet repayment' in which the principal amount is repaid in full in one sum at the very end of the term. Often, however, there is a prearranged repayment schedule (e.g. 20 percent of the principal each year for five years). This may be a preferable option to the borrower, as the decrease in the outstanding principal ensures that there is a corresponding decrease in the amount of interest paid. This is called 'amortisation'. In between these two is a 'balloon' where there are small amortisations and a large balancing capital repayment at maturity.

There are two main types of interest structure. Loans may be made at a fixed rate of interest which remains unchanged through the term of the loan, or at a variable rate of interest (a 'floating rate'), in which case the rate is adjusted periodically (perhaps every three, six or twelve months) in line with movements in money-market interest rates. The cost of floating rate loans is usually quoted as a margin over LIBOR, while for fixed rate loans, the rate quoted will be one figure which reflects an element of profit to cover the bank's credit risk on the borrower.

Security is the banker's second source of repayment in case a company hits trading difficulties or for other reasons cannot pay back the loan. The security may be property, or stocks and shares, or a guarantee from the directors, or a debenture. In the case of very large public companies it may be possible to lend on an unsecured basis on the principle that it would take a fairly major reverse to destroy one of the top 100 companies in the United Kingdom, whereas the future trading of a small company over the next five to ten years is obviously more uncertain.

Property is an ideal form of security, as it is an unchanging fixed asset which is easily valued and which should at least maintain its value. The bank will ensure that the borrower adequately insures the property (so that if it should burn down or be destroyed, the insurance proceeds should be sufficient to repay the loan) and the borrower has to undertake to maintain the property in good condition. There will usually be a covenant specifying a minimum ratio between the professional valuation of the property and the amount of the loan.

As mentioned above, the borrower in most cases has to make a number of undertakings to the bank as well. This can be seen as an additional form of security in as much that the borrower will agree to maintain a certain value in itself/its balance sheet (its 'net tangible worth') or will agree to keep its profits at a level sufficient to cover interest payments to the bank, say, three times over. These give the bank satisfaction of knowing that the borrower will be strong enough to weather any downturns and that, should it not, the bank then has the right to call for repayment of the loan at once.

At the end of the loan, the security would be released upon the successful repayment of the principal.

Over the term of the loan the borrower pays the bank interest on the outstanding principal (at the end of each interest period) but there are also various other further fees that are normally paid to a bank providing a medium-term loan. Some of these are as follows:

1. Arrangement fees (a one-off payment at the beginning of the loan to cover the bank's time and cost in providing the facility;
2. Commitment fees (which the borrower incurs by delaying taking the full principal),
3. Prepayment fees, incurred by repaying a proportion of the loan early.

The fee structure is very flexible and is one of the key points in the negotiation between the bank and the borrower.

When the terms of the loan have been agreed, the bank will draw up a formal agreement defining the terms and conditions (the facility letter or loan agreement) and will send that, and any other documents needed to perfect the security to the borrower for acceptance and return. Once the legal preliminaries have been fulfilled, the borrower will instruct the bank that it wishes to draw down the principal on a given date and will set the first interest period. The borrower will then remit funds to cover interest repayments and eventually the full principal as appropriate.

Syndicated bank lending

This outline has so far concentrated on medium-term lending where one bank lends directly to one borrower ('bilateral lines'). However, in cases where the amount required is larger than any given bank could make available, the funds would be raised by syndication.

The internal structure of the loan is virtually the same, although in this case one bank ('the arranger' or the 'lead bank') will carry out the discussions with the borrower and finalise the terms and conditions. At that point the arranger will speak to a number of banks and will invite them to lend a proportion of the total amount on the agreed terms. Participants will receive the interest payments from the borrower on their participation, and, in addition, will share the arrangement fee. Usually the arranger will keep the lion's share of the fee and each participant bank will receive a proportion of it, progressively larger in line with the size of its participation. Often participants will be given titles to reflect the amount of their participation such as Lead Manager, Co-manager, Manager, or Participant.

Over the term of the loan the arranging bank will act as Agent to the syndicate, monitoring the loan's covenants, routing the payments between borrower and banks, and maintaining liaison with the borrower. For this a small, annual agency fee is paid by the borrower for the Agent's own account.

When a syndicated loan is successfully completed an advertisement is usually placed in the financial press announcing broad details and the names of the parties involved. These are known as 'tombstones'.

The medium-term debt market

Two trends have characterised medium-/long-term bank debt markets in the 1980s: the emergence of the multi-option facility (or 'MOF') and 'disintermediation'.

Disintermediation is a clumsy word for a simple concept: rather than an investor making a deposit with a bank which then on-lends those funds to a borrower, why should the investor himself not purchase an instrument (a bond) directly from the borrower, cutting out the intermediary? This process, also called securitisation, was hit by the October 1987 stock-market crash, to the renewed benefit of lending banks.

The second concept, the MOF, is where a major borrower seeks to have a single facility which rolls up all its working capital needs. In an MOF a range of options is available to obtain funds in a range of currencies, or by acceptances from a syndicate of banks.

Typically, the banks in the syndicate will be in two layers. The first layer are the tender panel banks who have the right, but not the obligation, to make advances. Each time the borrower wishes to draw the Agent will invite the tender panel members to make bids below a specified margin over the cost of funds (called 'the cap'). The banks bidding most aggressively then lend for the fixed period requested, at the end of which the process is, if necessary, repeated.

Should there be no bids, or bids in an insufficient amount, then the second tier of banks, the underwriting banks, are obliged to lend at the cap. For this obligation they will receive, in addition to any income from lending when called upon to do so, a commitment commission.

The MOF has meant that the major borrower can secure finance at exceptionally fine rates. Banks usually claim that their participation in a MOF is for 'relationship purposes', that is to say that often the MOF business is not worth doing on its own account, but given that a borrower's other main bankers are usually in the MOF, it is necessary to be in too, in order to complete more profitable bilateral deals in the future.

8

e~o

LONG-TERM AND PERMANENT FINANCE, MERGERS AND ACQUISITIONS

NICHOLAS CAIGER-SMITH

This chapter deals with three primary subjects of corporate finance: first, the introduction of a company to the public market-place through admission to The Stock Exchange (formally known as 'The International Stock Exchange of the United Kingdom and the Republic of Ireland Limited'); secondly, the raising of additional long-term capital in the form of equity, debt or other marketable instruments; and thirdly, the business of 'mergers and acquisitions' (M&A), which covers acquisitions and divestments of companies, including company takeovers and mergers.

All three subjects represent major events for a public company. While its commercial operations are naturally its chief concern, it must also operate effectively in the financial markets, in which its shareholders and creditors assess its performance and its competitive position may be strengthened by the astute raising of capital or its acquisition or disposal of businesses.

An independent financial adviser, often a merchant bank with broad experience of clients and of the financial markets, may make an important contribution to the company's competitive success. The activities covered in this chapter are the core business of a merchant bank's 'corporate finance division'. A corporate finance division's work is mainly, but far from exclusively, financial and it typically employs banking, accounting, law or relevant industry skills.

Flotations

A company's admission to The Stock Exchange is known as a 'flotation'. The merchant bank's role is to sponsor the company's listing and its initial raising of capital and to handle many aspects of the preparatory work.

A company 'comes to the market', or is 'floated', with the aim of creating a market in its securities. It is likely to do this in order to raise additional capital; initially, this will probably be equity (share capital) since that is the core of any company's finance. An alternative aim may be to enable existing shareholders to sell their equity to outside investors. Through flotation, the company may extend its sources of finance from the private sources it has depended on until now, which include banks, to a larger pool of individual investors and, most importantly, institutional investors. This last category includes insurance companies, pension funds and investment trusts.

In coming to the market, the company is seeking a 'listing', or quotation of market prices for its securities. For a full listing, the company must meet certain criteria set down by The Stock Exchange in *Admission of Securities to Listing* ('the Yellow Book') and by the Companies Act 1985 and Financial Services Act 1986. These include a proven record, sound management, a suitable corporate and capital structure, and an expected market value of at least £700,000. The company will also be required to comply with continuing regulations regarding public disclosure of information about its business (not only in published accounts) to ensure the prompt release of information which may materially affect the market in its quoted securities or their pricing.

Through a quotation, a company may achieve one or more of several objectives, the major ones being; to extend its shareholder or lender base, so lessening dependence on existing ones; to raise new capital; to realise value for existing shareholders; to reduce its financing costs; to gain the ability to use listed securities as currency to pay for acquisitions; and ultimately to establish its continuing identity, independent of its founding members.

The role of the merchant bank

Ideally, the bank will have had a close relationship with the company before the flotation takes place. It will advise on the market for any securities to be issued; the terms, timing and amount of any issue; and the optimal financing structure, such as whether the company should sell only equity and in what form, or seek to raise debt also. The documentation is handled largely by the bank, which will have extensive professional experience in this area. The bank will lend its own reputation to the issue (a factor which may influence a potential investor's decision to purchase the securities to be issued) and the bank may also put itself financially at risk by underwriting an issue.

A flotation demands much preparation. For the company, it is a major event which may affect its structure, management, performance prospects and strategy. For the bank, which may offer its experience on all of these, the work also entails preparation of a prospectus. Working with accountants and lawyers, the bank must prepare a thorough, accurate and well-presented prospectus for investors, setting out all the information required to enable a potential investor to reach a fully-informed view of the company and its prospects as an investment. While the contents of the prospectus are governed by many laws and regulations, the issue of a prospectus is essentially a marketing exercise.

Methods of flotation

Three principal methods exist for floating a company on The Stock Exchange.

First, and most familiar to the public, is the *offer for sale*. This is the method which must be used for issues with an expected value of over £15 million and the offer is directed at both institutional and individual investors. It is the means by which many public-sector industries in the United Kingdom have been sold, such as British Telecom and British Gas.

The bank agrees, for a commission, to be the purchaser of last resort of shares in the company at a certain price, either from the company (if the company issues new shares) or from the existing shareholders (where it is existing share capital that is sold publicly). This is called 'underwriting' and is described more fully below.

The second and most commonly-used method is a *placing*. The bank subscribes for the securities, or agrees to purchase them in the last resort, under a placing agreement and immediately seeks to place them with investors, usually institutional ones. The Stock Exchange most commonly permits a placing where insufficient public interest may exist in the securities to be sold. A placing may be permitted where the expected value of the issue is less than £15 million.

The third method, an *introduction*, may be the chosen method of listing for a company whose equity is already widely held by public investors, such as a company already listed on another major stock exchange. (About two-thirds of the total market value of companies listed on The Stock Exchange represents the market value of companies also listed overseas.) An introduction may also be appropriate for a large company with sufficiently diverse a register of shareholders that listing would involve no change in its share capital or shareholders. An introduction does not entail a new issue of share capital – although it may sometimes follow a private placing of shares by a company.

Flotation on the Unlisted Securities Market and the Third Market

In addition to the 'full listing' on The Stock Exchange described above, two new markets have been created by The Stock Exchange to provide a market place in which smaller companies may raise capital: the Unlisted Securities Market (the USM), set up by The Stock Exchange in 1980, and the Third Market, opened in 1987. Both fall under The Stock Exchange's jurisdiction. They are still relatively small: in 1988 the market value of companies with full listing on The Stock Exchange was about £1300 billion (2,700 companies), while that of USM companies was less than £8 billion (some 400 companies) and that of the Third Market only £400 million (approximately 50 companies).

Similar listing procedures apply for the USM and Third Market as for a full listing but certain conditions are less stringent. A quotation on the USM is open to a company with only three years' trading history (a full listing, by contrast, requires five); a company is not obliged to put more than 10 percent of its equity in public hands (as against 25 percent for a full listing); and there are in principle no minimum size restrictions.

The Third Market was conceived as a public venture-capital market to provide a means to launch small, young companies with rapid growth prospects. Many such companies first began life with private financing from venture-capital funds. The requirements for joining the Third Market are still less onerous than for the USM. Start-up ventures may be admitted without audited accounts, although normally audited accounts for at least one full year must be available. The continuing guidance of the sponsor is sought to ensure the best prospects for the success of newly-launched companies.

The normal method of launching a company on the Third Market is by a placing, as the typical entrant is a high-risk venture in which only specialist institutions and funds are likely to invest.

Pricing and Underwriting

Pricing is one of the most important aspects of a new issue and can often be the most difficult. The sellers of securities – the company issuing new shares, existing shareholders or a combination of both – naturally want the highest price; the investors want an attractively low price. The bank's goal is to obtain the best value for the seller commensurate with ensuring that the investors feel that they have made a sound investment both at the time of purchase and after a period of being invested.

The bank must usually, therefore, stand between buyer and seller. It undertakes both the pricing and the sale of the securities. Before the issue takes place, the bank underwrites the issue, guaranteeing to the seller that all securities will be purchased at a determined price. The bank itself is thus liable to purchase any securities not sold at the end of the offer (or placing) period.

In the case of an offer for sale, but not a placing, the bank usually arranges to offset its underwriting liability by assembling, with the assistance of a stockbroker, a group of sub-underwriters who are usually large institutional investors. These enter into an agreement with the bank, similar to the bank's agreement with the original seller; each commits to purchase, if called upon to do so, a portion of the issue and for assuming this risk receives a sub-underwriting commission from the bank. Usually, underwriters and sub-underwriters do not expect to be called upon to meet their obligations, but in some cases (such as the sale of Government-owned shares in BP in October 1987) they may have to do so.

In a placing, the underwriting process is simpler: the bank, again with the assistance of a stockbroker, identifies a select group of interested investors. The need for a public marketing exercise or for sub-underwriting is obviated.

A bank's ability to line up sub-underwriters for a large offer, or placees for a placing, depends in part on its record in pricing issues. When dealings begin, an issue may be deemed poorly priced, and therefore unsuccessful, *either* because dealings open at a large premium, suggesting that the seller has not received a reasonable price for his securities *or* because lack of demand sends the price to a discount, leaving the purchasers (and possibly the underwriters) with an unrealised loss.

Pricing difficulty is especially acute in volatile markets. One method, still unusual, that allows a flexible approach to pricing in these circumstances, or where a company's business is exceptionally difficult to value, is the sale by tender. This is effectively an auction to the public. The offer is not made at a pre-determined price; instead, applicants are invited to state the price they are willing to pay and the issue is allotted to the highest bidders.

Privatisations

Recent privatisations of public-sector industry in the United Kingdom represent a special case of flotation business, owing to their size, complexity and political dimension. Although privatised industries come to the market from public (i.e. Government) ownership, many of the key financial issues are nevertheless identical to those relating to the quotation of a company of privately-owned origin. Certain merchant banks have had prominent roles in advising either the Government or the company being privatised and have developed relevant specialist expertise. This is increasingly in demand overseas as other governments pursue privatisation programmes.

The difficulties of pricing new issues have been well aired during the Government's privatisation programme. They include uncertainty as to the level of demand for the issue and as to investors' perception of the unusual features of certain privatised industries (for example, dominant market positions which are suddenly opened to new competitive pressures). The general public and the media have identified themselves with both the seller (through the Government's public ownership) and the buyer (as prospective shareholders).

Raising additional capital

A quotation opens the way to a company to raise capital on The Stock Exchange, USM or Third Market through further issues of equity, debt or some variant of either.

A company may issue further equity for cash or as consideration for assets or for the share capital of an acquired company. Cash may be required to provide working capital, to invest in the business or to fund an acquisition. The Companies Act 1985 generally requires equity issues for cash to be offered by way of rights to existing shareholders – a 'rights issue'. Normally made at a discount to the current share price and frequently underwritten, a rights issue usually assures the issuing company a secure capital-raising without major change in the pattern of the company's shareholders.

Institutional investors support rights issues because of the discount and the underwriting opportunities, while issuing companies value them because they help to preserve stability in their shareholder registers.

Issues of equity in exchange for assets or a company's share capital are an important method of financing company acquisitions, which are described in more detail below.

Equity normally takes the form of ordinary shares, on which the dividend payable is at the discretion of a company's directors. A less common form of equity which has recently gained favour with issuers, especially companies making acquisitions, is the convertible preference share. The dividend payable on a preference share (whether a convertible one or not) is fixed and is more secure than the dividend on an ordinary share, and therefore provides an investor with income similar to that of a debt instrument. Further, a convertible preference share is convertible into ordinary shares and is therefore classed under company law as equity, not debt. The combination of these two features enables a company making an acquisition to offer securities which, for investors, have the fixed-income attractions of a debt investment, while at the same time augmenting the company's equity base rather than its borrowings, leaving its balance sheet stronger.

Debt securities may be issued either for cash or to finance the purchase of assets or the share capital of an acquired company. Long-term debt tends to bear a fixed interest rate. The terms 'fixed interest' and 'fixed-income' have thus come to be applied often loosely to all kinds of stocks and bonds evidencing any form of debt.

Debt in the form of marketable loan stock may be either unsecured or secured (by a floating charge on the company's assets or, often in the case of property companies, by a fixed charge on specified assets). Such loan stocks tend to have a term of at least 15 years. For shorter-term debt-raisings, companies usually borrow from banks or issue bonds in the Euromarkets, referred to below.

Convertible loan stock enables certain companies to raise debt on finer terms than simple loan stock. Convertible loan stock is a debt instrument which pays interest but has the additional feature that over a period of years the stock may be converted into the company's shares at a given conversion price, almost always higher than prevails for the shares at the time the stock is issued. If the company's growth prospects are good, investors will be willing to pay for this feature by accepting a reduced interest rate on the stock while it remains unconverted.

Loan stocks may also be issued with warrants attached, which entitle the holder to purchase the company's shares at a pre-determined price, either for a cash payment or upon surrender of the loan stocks themselves. Again, the conversion feature has a value to investors who hope subsequently to purchase the underlying equity on attractive terms; this helps to reduce the interest rate carried by the stock. Further, warrants may be detached and separately traded, widening the potential market for the company's shares.

Since the 1960s, more and more companies have turned to the international 'Euromarkets' to raise debt and, more recently, equity and derivatives of equity. The Euromarkets are less regulated and allow a wider pool of capital to be tapped in more varied ways than do the public markets in the United Kingdom, though The Stock Exchange remains one of the world's largest regulated exchanges for dealings in companies' securities.

Mergers and acquisitions

Mergers and acquisitions have increasingly captured the public attention. A period of economic expansion in the world, the economic benefits gained from the consolidation of industries and the deregulation of financial and commercial markets have all contributed to intensified corporate M&A activity.

The combination of two companies through a merger or takeover may affect not only investors in either company but also the companies' competitors, customers and employees, and perhaps society at large. As a result, in the United Kingdom such transactions have become increasingly complex and highly regulated. The role of merchant banks has grown in importance. A merchant bank will advise on some or all of a range of related matters, including strategy, acquisition opportunities, negotiation tactics, financing and defence against a hostile bid. It will often act for its clients in negotiations. It also co-ordinates the various professionals (lawyers, accountants, etc.) who are always involved and provides guidance through the regulatory aspects of such transactions.

Types of M&A and the making of offers

Types of M&A include agreed private acquisitions of companies or assets; public takeovers, which are usually agreed but may involve a hostile offer to a company's shareholders against the will of its management; and true mergers, which involve the creation of a new company out of two (or more).

Such transactions are proposed for many different reasons, but to succeed in the longer run they must be founded on some commercial justification. The proposing company's strategic aim is to improve its competitive situation: by integrating vertically or horizontally, expanding geographically, increasing market share, rationalising its activities or purchasing poorly-managed assets to manage them better. Sometimes this motivation may be defensive, as when a company that feels its position to be weak seeks a stronger partner of its own choosing.

In a public takeover, the key tactical aim of an offeror (the company making the offer) is to secure acceptance of the offer in respect of over 50 percent of the voting capital of the offeree (the company to be acquired). This gives the offeror voting control. A secondary aim may be to obtain over 90 percent of the offeree's voting capital – company law then permits the offeror to acquire compulsorily any remainder.

Most takeovers proceed on the basis of an agreement between the management of the two companies as to price and other terms, and the management of the offeree is therefore able to recommend to its shareholders that they accept the offeror's offer. Similarly, mergers are usually proposed to shareholders of the participating companies by their managements on pre-agreed terms. In either case, negotiation of terms is likely to involve a bank.

In a small minority of cases, an offer by one company to acquire another may be announced on a hostile basis. A bank's experience of such difficult situations and the professional and media contacts it has developed may confer significant advantage to either the offeror or offeree company. Such a bid may develop into a fierce battle for the support of the offeree's shareholders, fought through the official mechanisms of offer document and defence document, through the media and even at a political level. (The competing bids by Nestlé and Suchard for Rowntree and Minorco's bid for Consolidated Goldfields, all in 1988, may be familiar examples.)

Methods of defence

A hostile offeror has the advantage of holding the initiative in an unpredictable situation. The eventual success of its offer, however, depends chiefly on the price offered and the commercial and managerial justification.

Offeree companies have developed various tactics to evade unwelcome offers. The key objectives are to persuade shareholders that the offer is too low and to challenge the commercial justification for the offer. Where the offeror offers equity rather than cash as consideration, the offeree's management will argue to its shareholders that equity in their existing company will be a more attractive investment than equity in the offeror should the takeover succeed. Other defensive tactics include management buy-outs or the introduction of a 'white knight'.

Management buy-outs have developed in the United Kingdom since 1985, based on American practices. A company's management may respond to an offer for the company by itself making a competing, and more attractive, offer to shareholders, typically heavily financed by borrowings from banks and institutions.

Alternatively, the offeree's management may seek a 'white knight' – a preferred offeror which not only will offer a higher price than the initial offeror but also is more sympathetic to existing management and its strategy. An offer from a 'white knight' would be recommended to shareholders by the offeree's management.

Regulation of takeovers and mergers

The conduct of takeovers and mergers is supervised by the Panel on Takeovers and Mergers. The Panel was established in the late 1960s, largely at the instigation of City organisations. It represents a 'watchdog' and an informal court of appeal on the conduct of takeovers and mergers. It has its own professional staff and the full Panel itself comprises leading City representatives.

The Panel's *'City Code on Takeovers and Mergers'* is a rule-book which sets down principles to be followed by offeror and offeree companies and their advisers. The Code does not have the force of law and, when points of law are at issue, parties may resort to legal action. However, together with company law, the Financial Services Act 1986 and Stock Exchange regulations, the Code provides a regulatory framework which governs all takeovers and mergers.

Company law restricts the extent of ownership that one company may acquire in another, without public disclosure, to 5 percent of the voting capital. This is currently under review and may be lowered. The Code sets limits on how much voting capital a company may purchase in another company before making an offer for it, or early in the offer period. It controls tightly the nature, presentation and timing of information to be provided to shareholders by both offeror and offeree companies, and requires disclosure when different organisations work in concert with one another. It restricts the kinds of action an offeree company may take to evade its being acquired. It also requires an offeree company (and an offeror in a reverse takeover) to obtain competent independent advice. The ultimate aim is to ensure that the interests of shareholders are safeguarded and that takeovers and mergers are pursued without unfair advantage to either side.

The effects of takeovers and mergers are overseen by the Office of Fair Trading, which may decide to refer a proposed merger or offer to the Monopolies and Mergers Commission (the MMC). (Recent examples include the reference of Minorco's bid for Consolidated Goldfields, and GEC and Siemens' bid for Plessey.) The MMC will rule on whether or not a proposed merger or takeover would result in an unacceptable concentration of market share in the industry, or other undesirable consequences. Reference of a bid to the MMC causes it to lapse and many bids are not subsequently revived.

As a result of both tighter regulation and the increase in M&A activity, M&A business has grown in complexity and few transactions proceed perfectly smoothly. A merchant bank that has experience of implementing different financing methods and knowledge of its clients' businesses and their management is able to advise on tactics throughout an offer period and can competently co-ordinate all the parties involved.

9

❧

PRIVATISATION

LYNDA ROUSE

Privatisation can take a number of forms, but the most important privatisation transactions culminate in offers for sale to the public of shares in substantial companies, often household names. The first such issue, of 51 percent of British Aerospace, took place in February 1981. The Government's privatisation programme built up slowly at first, but by the late 1980s was raising around £5 billion per year for the Exchequer.

Privatisations often grab the headlines at the time of flotation. However, intensive programmes of work over many months, and sometimes years, lead up to these public offers, involving large teams of professional advisers working with Government officials and the managements of the businesses themselves. Merchant banks play a central role in these preparations. Although the end product is usually a conventional merchant banking transaction (i.e. a flotation on The Stock Exchange), many aspects of the merchant banks' roles in privatisation are unique to this type of work.

A feature of privatisation issues in the United Kingdom is that they involve at least two merchant banks and supporting advisory teams. This was not so in the early days. In the flotation of British Aerospace, a single merchant bank advised both the Government (as vendor of the shares on offer) and the company itself. However, these two parties had conflicting interests in a number of important areas (the structure of the new company's balance sheet, the proportion of privatisation proceeds to be retained by the business, and so on). These pressures led to the practice of each party – the Government as vendor and the business itself – seeking independent advice from its own merchant bank, broker, lawyers and accountants.

Later, when the practice of offering tranches of shares in the United States was adopted, a US sponsoring bank was required, with three US legal advisers (advising the vendor, the company and the US sponsor). The US lawyers' role is to ensure the correct harmonisation of the very different flotation procedures used in the United Kingdom and the United States. This development has greatly complicated the process and added to the complexity of the advisory role.

The proliferation of advice on privatisation issues took a new turn with the decision to undertake simultaneous offers for sale of the ten water authorities and the twelve area electricity boards. In these cases, merchant banks were appointed to advise the Government (as vendor), the industry as a whole (on matters in its collective interest) and the companies individually. The corporate finance departments of almost all of the major merchant banks are thus heavily involved in privatisation, and privatisation issues require very large meeting rooms indeed.

The merchant banks' advisory role

Once the Government has decided that the privatisation of a particular business is politically desirable, it then has to decide whether it is feasible. Merchant banks are often appointed to advise at this very early stage, which might precede flotation by a number of years.

Deciding on the feasibility of a particular privatisation is not just a matter of assessing the financial prospects of the business. Changes are often needed in its commercial environment (its relationships with its suppliers, customers and competitors) or in its regulatory environment (controlling any potential abuse of monopoly or near monopoly power in its market), in order to fit it for the private sector. In some cases, functions which would be inappropriate for private sector companies have had to be separated, or social responsibilities have had to be explicitly defined and enshrined in operating licences. In other cases, state-owned businesses have been completely restructured before privatisation, or created for the purpose from what were previously essentially Government departments. The merchant banks need to ensure that any proposed new arrangements of this sort are consistent with the successful privatisation of the business. Only when the overall strategy is in place, and the resulting prospects for the business can be assessed, can the feasibility of privatisation be established.

Once a privatisation strategy has been agreed, it has to be implemented. This involves two strands of work. The first revolves around the legislative process. Most nationalised industries are established by statute: if part or all of such business is to be privatised, new powers are needed to restructure the business as necessary, to create a new public limited company with the necessary share capital (owned initially by the appropriate Secretary of State), and to enable the Secretary of State to sell his shares.

In addition, if the privatised business is to be regulated, legislation is needed to confer the necessary powers on the Secretary of State and the Regulator, backed by a draft operating licence for the business which has to be subject to Parliamentary scrutiny. While most of this work is done within Government, the merchant banks play an important role in ensuring that the legislative position is consistent with a successful flotation. For example, the tax position of the new company created by legislation, its capital structure and regulatory environment are important factors in its flotation prospects.

The second strand of work is associated with implementing any restructuring needed before privatisation. Sometimes new companies need to be formed from parts of nationalised industries; in other cases new subsidiaries need to be created. Almost always, management and organisational changes are undertaken to ensure that the business is ready for a new environment and new responsibilities. In some cases, new contracts with suppliers or customers are needed and in others, the business has to be adapted to work within an entirely new regulatory regime. Where substantial change is effected, the new arrangements have to be established well before flotation. Potential investors need to be able to assess the financial record of the business in its new form before they make their investment decisions. The merchant banks are closely involved with this part of the work programme and, in almost all cases, these tasks are undertaken within an extremely tight timetable. This type of involvement in the Government's privatisation programme has led the merchant banks to build up skills very different from those required in their more traditional corporate finance work.

Once the new public limited company is established in its new environment, the emphasis of the advisory work switches to the flotation itself. Now the merchant banks find themselves on more familiar ground although, as will become clear, privatisation issues even at this stage have a number of unusual characteristics.

Many of the unusual features of privatisation issues arise because they are so large. The British Telecommunications (BT) flotation was, at that time in December 1984, not simply the biggest ever attempted in the United Kingdom, but the biggest world-wide by a significant factor. It is no exaggeration to say that privatisation has transformed the new issue market in the United Kingdom. Private sector companies obtaining a Stock Exchange listing for the first time by means of an offer for sale usually offer less than 30 percent of their shares to the public and rarely raise more than £100 million by this means. Notable exceptions were Reuters £205 million in 1984; Abbey Life £240 million in 1985; 1986 was an exceptional year in which Wellcome raised £253 million, Morgan Grenfell raised £160 million and Avis (Europe) raised £180 million; and Eurotunnel raised £770 million in 1987. By contrast the Government must dispose of at least 51 percent of a state-owned business before this 'counts' as a privatisation. Increasingly, the trend has been to dispose of 100 percent in a single sale, even when the amounts of money involved have been very substantial (see Table 9.1).

Some of the so-called secondary privatisation offers (i.e. offers of the Government's residual holdings in privatised and other private sector companies) have also been very large as is shown in Table 9.2.

By contrast, new shares in listed companies are only rarely offered for sale to the general public outside the privatisation arena. When companies themselves come to the stock market, existing shareholders have what are called pre-emption rights, which allow them preferential access to these rights issues.

Table 9.1. Privatisation new issues

		Money raised (£)	Proportion of the shares offered for sale (%)
1981	British Aerospace	150m	51
	Cable & Wireless	224m	51
1982	Britoil	549m	51
1984	Enterprise Oil	392m	100
	Jaguar	294m	100
	British Telecom	3,916m	51
1986	British Gas	5,434m	100
	Trustee Savings Bank*	1,495m	100
1987	British Airways	900m	100
	Rolls Royce	1,363m	100
	British Airports	1,225m	100
1988	British Steel	2,500m	100

* Not strictly a privatisation issue, although the offer was Government inspired.

Table 9.2. Secondary privatisation offers

		£m
1979	British Petroleum	290
1983	British Petroleum	566
	Cable & Wireless	275
1985	British Aerospace	551
	Britoil	449
	Cable & Wireless*	933
1987	British Petroleum	7,240

* Part of this issue was of new shares offered by the company itself to its existing shareholders.

Wider share ownership

Another unusual aspect of privatisation issues is the involvement of individual, as opposed to institutional, investors. Before the advent of privatisation, individuals' interest in the equity market had been in decline. The institutions – pension funds, insurance companies, etc. – had accounted for the major part of new equity investment for many years, while individuals had been net sellers. Most individuals who owned shares in 1979 had held them for a considerable period: many had acquired them by inheritance. Thus, individual investors were of almost negligible importance in new issues. The sheer size of privatisation issues made it essential to tap a much wider market and individual investors became increasingly important in this respect.

The early privatisation issues demonstrated that small investors were interested in this type of investment. However, some of the smaller issues (Amersham 1982, Associated British Ports 1983) were substantially oversubscribed, with two adverse effects on individual investors. First, many subscribers were very discouraged by lack of success in the ballots which were needed to allocate shares in these issues. Secondly, many of the people who were successful in the ballots found the temptation to sell at a considerable premium irresistible. Small investors acquired the art of stagging (i.e. subscribing for new issues where demand was strong, with the intention of selling soon after at a considerable profit), often with overdrafts specifically provided for the purpose by their local bank managers. Neither of these developments was helpful to the Government's aspirations for wider share ownership.

To encourage long-term equity investment by private individuals, the merchant banking advisers on the 1982 Britoil issue devised a loyalty bonus. Small investors were offered one bonus share for each ten still held at the end of three years. The choice of issue for this innovation was unfortunate since, for various reasons, the issue flopped. It was to be some time before the share price returned to the level of the issue price. This was probably a more potent factor than the loyalty bonus in encouraging long-term ownership by the small-scale investors who had originally subscribed. However, the device has been used successfully in subsequent issues.

In later issues, participation by individuals was specifically encouraged by major publicity campaigns and, in the case of retail businesses, incentives for customer shareholders. In many cases, special offices were established to oversee the wide dissemination of information to individuals thinking of applying for shares. The merchant banks have found themselves paying increasing attention to this aspect of privatisation transactions.

The use of television advertising began with the Cable & Wireless issue in 1983. However, it was a much more important component of the very large offer of 51 percent of British Telecommunications in 1984. Before the issue, there were serious doubts about the ability of UK institutions to raise the £4 billion required, so private and overseas investors were seen to be crucial to its success. This was as much a matter of sheer practicality as of political desirability. Indeed, the cynical would say that the political dimension was conferred after the event. The programme of advertising and incentives devised for individual investors by the merchant banks and public relations advisers, including the use of a simplified 'mini prospectus' was certainly very successful. There were about 2 million successful applications by small investors, half of whom had never owned shares before, a performance which greatly surprised most professional observers of the UK stock market.

The targeting of individual investors is now a routine part of privatisation issues, particularly the larger ones. The marketing programme used for British Gas ('if you see Sid, tell him') typified the Government's message that investing in privatisation issues is for everyone. For much of the period after BT, these marketing efforts were aided by the very strong performance of the stock market. However, the stock market crash in October 1987 coincided with the very large offer of British Petroleum (BP) shares. Many small investors responded to the advertising slogan 'be part of it', even when it was clear that the issue would flop. The subsequent poor performance of the stock market badly affected privatisation portfolios, further discouraging small investors. The market was tested only once in the year after the crash, with the privatisation of British Steel in difficult market conditions at the end of 1988. Perhaps surprisingly, this issue attracted some 500,000 small investors.

Other unusual features

From the point of view of the merchant banks, privatisation issues have a number of other unusual features. For example, pricing of the issues is done in the knowledge that the Public Accounts Committee (an all-party committee of MPs) will subsequently report on the issue, with hindsight and with a view to ensuring that the taxpayer obtained fair value for the shareholding. This puts even more pressure than usual on those charged with the difficult task of pricing these very large issues, often in industries where no private sector comparators exist.

The logistics of very large issues targeted on small investors raise substantial complications for the merchant banks, as well as for the receiving bankers and the companies' registrars. So too does the practice of offering employees preferential treatment in privatisation issues. Merchant bankers face few other situations in which they are required to make presentations on transactions to meetings of shop stewards.

The underwriting of privatisation issues started in a manner quite similar to that of other offers for sale. The lead bank (in this case, the merchant bank to the Government) arranged the underwriting, using a small syndicate to spread the risk in larger transactions. As the issues grew larger, the net widened. In the BT issue, almost every major merchant bank in the City was involved in the underwriting. Since the Government (unlike most users of the capital market) was the source of a substantial and continuing volume of underwriting business, it found itself able to drive down underwriting fees and to introduce competition for participation in underwriting syndicates. Following the diffi-cult issue of BP shares in 1987, where the underwriters' interests departed substantially from those of the Government (in that the underwriters would have avoided substantial losses had the issue been withdrawn when market conditions suddenly deteriorated), the Government announced that its future policy would be to bar its merchant bank and the merchant bank adviser to the company in future issues from the position of lead underwriter. This consti-tutes a very significant departure from normal non-privatisation practice.

Privatisation and the London capital market

Two ways in which privatisation has changed the London capital market have been mentioned. Perceptions of the appetite of the market for new issues have been transformed and the interest of individual investors in equity issues has been greatly stimulated. A third effect has been a significant increase in the choice of UK equities now available for investment. Whole new sectors have been created (telecommunications, airports), and very substantial companies (e.g. British Gas, British Aerospace, British Steel) have been added to investors' lists. As the privatisation programme moved into the area of utilities (water, electricity), the process significantly enhanced the supply of safe income stocks available on the London market, thereby adding further to investor choice.

10

◦❦◦

INTERNATIONAL CAPITAL MARKETS

NIGEL C. À BRASSARD

The international capital markets comprise a number of different sectors which fall broadly into two categories. The first are the number of domestic capital markets in which foreign borrowers issue securities. The second is the Eurobond market in which securities are issued and placed largely outside the country of domicile of the issuer.

Both these international markets have their roots in the issues of securities by governments and corporations in domestic capital markets other than their own. After the Second World War a number of European governments issued debt in the US capital market. This market was attractive to them because the disclosure requirements were not too onerous, relatively large amounts could be raised and the dollar was regarded as an internationally accepted currency. Along with this demand from borrowers to issue, there was an increasing demand from investors to purchase these securities. Whilst these investors were largely domestic, increasingly interest was shown by investors outside the United States.

The growth of the international markets over the last few decades has been phenomenal. The debt and equity securities issued in the international capital markets are issued by supranational organisations, governments and government agencies, industrial and commercial companies and financial institutions. UK issuers accounted for approximately 130 issues which raised in excess of $21 billion in 1988.

The principal types of securities offered in the international capital markets are as follows:

1. *Foreign Bonds* are fixed rate debt securities issued by foreign borrowers in the domestic market of the other countries. They are typically underwritten and sold by domestic banks in the country of issue and denomination in that country's currency. Foreign bonds issued in the United States are known as Yankee bonds, in Japan as Samurai bonds and in London as Bulldog bonds.
2. *Eurobonds* are debt securities with a fixed or floating rate of interest which are underwritten by an international syndicate of banks and which are sold

to investors principally outside the country of the currency in which the securities are denominated. In recent years the majority of issues have been denominated in US dollars, yen, Deutschmarks, sterling, European Currency Units, Australian and Canadian dollars. Eurobonds can be issued for maturities of one year to twenty years or longer, but the majority of issues are for periods of five to ten years. Unlike the domestic capital markets, the Euromarket has no market-place: trading of issues takes place in an international over-the-counter market. Typically, issues are listed on an internationally recognised stock exchange. The first Eurobond issue was launched in 1963 in response to the effective closure of the US domestic capital market to foreign borrowers as a result of the imposition of the Interest Equalisation Tax.

3. *International equity issues* Since the mid 1980s an international equity market has developed for the following reasons:

    (a) deregulation of financial markets and the ending of exchange controls, which have facilitated cross-border flows of equity;

    (b) increasing use of global stock indices to measure portfolio performance;

    (c) privatisation programmes, which have in many instances required international demand to supplement the domestic market;

    (d) advances in computers, communications and other technologies which have assisted in the process of 24-hour trading in securities;

    (e) increasing interest by companies in issuing new equity and broadening their shareholder base outside their home market.

An international equity issue involves the distribution of a company's equity to investors in a number of countries outside the company's home market. The underwriting and distribution techniques used are similar to those used for the issue of Eurobonds, so these issues are also known as Euro-equity issues. The international issue can be in conjunction with an issue in the domestic market, or may be entirely separate.

1. *Euroconvertibles* are of fixed rate securities which can be exchanged at any time during their life (typically to 15 years) for a pre-determined number of shares of the issuer, its parent or another company (the last are called exchangeable issues). The conversion is set at a premium to the share price at the time of issue. The Euroconvertible market has grown rapidly in the last five years, along with the expansion of the international equity market. The majority of issuers have been companies in the United States, Japan the United Kingdom and Australia. Whilst it is typical for the issue to be denominated in the same currency as that of the issuer's equity, there are many instances of convertibles being issued in a different currency.

2. *Eurobonds with equity warrants* comprise two separate elements. The first is a host bond which is a conventional fixed-rate Eurobond of typically five to seven years' maturity. The second component is an equity warrant, which

is a long-dated call option giving the holder the right to purchase a company's equity at a price which is fixed at the time of issue and which can be exercised at any time during the life of the bond. Issues have been made by a number of companies including many UK corporations, but in recent years the market has been denominated by Japanese companies who have accounted for over 90 percent of all issues.

Reasons for Issuing in the International Capital Markets

Borrowers will arrange issues of securities outside their domestic markets for a number of different reasons:

1. *Diversification* of their sources of finance. An issuer which has already raised debt or equities in its domestic market may wish to diversify its source of investors or shareholders.
2. *Cost* The international markets may be cheaper or more cost-effective than the domestic markets. The reasons for the difference in cost can be explained by tapping new demand for an issuer's securities or taking advantage of tax or regulatory differences.
3. *Less restrictive financial covenants* Often it will be a standard feature of domestic capital markets for there to be financial covenants associated with an issue. In general, the informational markets tend to be less insistent on financial covenants and most Eurobonds are issued with a negative pledge (restricting the issuer from granting security on future borrowings) as principal covenant.
4. *Different ratings* Frequently companies have been able to tap foreign markets where companies in a particular sector may be more highly rated than in their domestic market.
5. *Availability* At times it is possible for a borrower to arrange an issue in the international markets when it has not been possible in the issuer's domestic market. This may arise from a number of factors, including investor demand and fiscal or monetary constraints.
6. *Innovations* The Eurobond market has traditionally been receptive to new structures. These new structures can be developed to meet the specific demands of issuers or investors. This contrasts with many domestic markets, which tend to be less receptive to new structures for issues.
7. *Currency* An issuer may wish to raise borrowings in a foreign currency to hedge a foreign currency exposure.
8. *Efficiency* The Euromarket new issue process, including the documentation, syndication and distribution is simple and straightforward. This allows an issuer to tap 'market windows' at relatively short notice.
9. *Prestige and publicity* An issue in the international markets can be a useful exercise in increasing investor awareness for a company.

The Role of Accepting Houses in the International Capital Markets

Some of the accepting houses have been actively involved in the development of the international capital markets. The accepting houses are involved in the arrangement of new issues, underwriting of the securities, distribution of the issue to investors and making markets in the securities.

1. *Arrangement of new issues* Accepting houses will work with their clients in keeping them informed on a regular basis of the costs and opportunities for arranging an issue in the international capital markets. In addition, the accepting house will work with its clients to arrange an issue which meets specific financing requirements.
2. *Documentation* The lead manager assists the borrower with the preparation of a prospectus and the legal agreements necessary for the issue and for listing the securities.
3. *Underwriting of new issues* Accepting houses will, on their own or with a group of other securities houses, underwrite new issues. The lead manager typically forms the management syndicate, taking into account the distribution abilities and relationship factors.
4. *Distribution* Having underwritten a new issue, an accepting house would wish to distribute the securities as quickly as possible to its investor clients.
5. *Market-making* Investors usually require liquidity for their investments, that is they wish to be able to convert their investment into cash prior to the maturity of the issue. A number of banks, including some of the accepting houses, make markets in both debt and equity securities.

UK Companies and the International Capital Markets

Many of the leading UK companies have arranged issues in the international capital markets. The most frequent issuers have been the banks and building societies, although an increasing number of UK companies have now tapped the Euromarkets.

Issues have typically been for five to ten years and in amounts of £50 – 100 million. The majority of issues have been in the Eurosterling market. However, there have been a number of issues in foreign currencies. Some of these issues have been to hedge foreign currency exposures or to finance overseas operations. Other foreign currency issues have been swapped into sterling or another required currency.

In recent years, UK companies have been active in equity-linked Euromarkets, particularly through the issue of Euroconvertibles. The inclusion of an equity option has enabled smaller and less well-known companies to issue in the Euromarkets, some of which would not have been able to issue in the straight debt market.

11

◦∽◦

VENTURE CAPITAL

MARK O'HANLON

The phrase 'venture capital' refers to a very diverse and fragmented industry. It covers seed capital and start-up investments as well as £700 million management buy-outs. The diversity of the industry reflects both the evolution of methods of financing unquoted deals as well as the development of a more sophisticated appreciation of the risk-reward profile of investors and venture capitalists. The very nature of the industry has led to the increasing specialisation of the players in the market. Increasingly, many venture capital organisations as well as providers of funds are concentrating their efforts on 'development capital', such as large buy-outs and expansion finance, and eschewing start-up deals where the risks involved are too high and the skills required are unavailable. But some venture capital organisations still become involved in deals at all their different stages.

Venture capital funds raised in 1988 totalled just under £700 million, whilst the total amount of capital raised since the beginning of 1981 stands at £2.5 billion. It comes from traditional sources such as UK pension funds, UK life assurance companies and foreign institutions as well as from industrial corporations and private individuals (see Table 11.1).

Table 11.1. Providers of capital 1988

	£m
UK pension funds	226
UK insurance companies	86
Foreign institutions	156
UK fund management group	34
Industrial corporations	35
Other	162
Total	699

The specific venture capital organisations provide the management of these funds and are responsible for investing a dedicated pool of capital. These operations, in general, may be part of an institution such as a pension fund or they may be independent, managing money that they have raised from the institutions, usually in the form of closed-end funds. At the end of 1987 there were 107 such organisations with over £4 billion under management. Of this sum nearly £2.5 billion was managed by firms associated with institutions and £1.1 billion by independent firms. The remainder was managed by small groups, either working from within the public sector or by joint ventures in which the investment manager and a sponsoring organisation provided the capital.

In recent years the venture capital industry has seen a remarkable amount of activity from which clear trends can be seen. (Table 11.2 gives details of these trends.) Initially, in the early 1980s, venture capitalists concerned themselves more with early stage investments, particularly in the field of high technology start-ups. However, developments in the UK economy as well as the changing return requirements of the venture capitalists have shifted the emphasis away from this area to management buy-outs (MBOs). The pace of activity in this area has grown considerably over the last decade, with MBOs growing in number and value terms. In 1980, around 100 buy-outs were completed with a total value of some £40 million: by 1988 this had grown to 300 totalling £3.8 billion.

Table 11.2. UK investment by financing stage (% of amount invested)

Financing stage	1983	1987
Start-up	14.9	8.0
Early stage	10.3	4.2
Expansion	43.3	22.2
Buy-out/in	24.2	62.5
Other purchase	6.8	3.1
Other	0.5	—

Source: UK Venture Capital Journal

The largest buy-out to that point was the 1987 MFI deal, which involved a total consideration of £715 million. This growth in MBO activity has been stimulated by the dramatic upturn in corporate mergers and acquisitions during the period which, along with the increasing number of disposals of companies and divisions by larger corporate entities, has provided ample scope for management to purchase their own company.

A general political and fiscal atmosphere which encourages individuality and entrepreneurial drive has also played a significant part in fuelling this growth in buy-out activity.

A more recent development has been the rise in numbers of management buy-ins (MBIs). In an MBO the existing management or a team thereof combine with a venture capital group to buy the business they manage from its existing shareholders. However, in an MBI a management group which has nothing to do with the company is backed by a venture capitalist and buys in to the company. These deals are more similar to start-ups, in that the venture capital group has a greater risk as the new management team does not have the inside knowledge of the company which the existing management has. In 1988 some 40 MBIs were completed, totalling over £1 billion.

The venture capital industry in the United Kingdom is at present at a major crossroads. One of the most significant paradoxes which faces the industry is that the deals which generate the highest returns (particularly in terms of short pay-back periods) are the ones with the lowest risk profile. The industry is concentrating on MBOs, which of necessity involve profitable companies with secure cash flows which tend to operate in mature and stable markets. It has eschewed the smaller start-up deals because these are more risky and take longer to provide a return for the venture capitalist.

This rational decision was prompted by a need to safeguard the returns of the investors; however, it has increasingly led to capital crowding in the market and a resultant lowering of returns as more players chase after deals. In 1988 new equity funds launched raised new money totalling £370 million, whilst several mezzanine (high-yielding) funds have recently been launched. This surfeit of capital has meant that the traditional returns sought by venture capital groups, of say 30 percent per annum, are being significantly lowered.

One corollary of this is that some venture capitalists are looking beyond their traditional remit of purely unquoted companies towards other areas such as smaller quoted companies. It is felt that in this area returns can be safeguarded as the capital pressure is less and the stocks enjoy the benefits of liquidity. Bought deals have recently become popular, in which the venture capital organisation buys the company outright and either installs new management with a smaller stake in the company than is the norm, or keeps the existing team. The lead venture capitalist then syndicates the investment to lower his risk exposure.

Similarly, many UK venture capital organisations are looking to Europe for opportunities. Europe has traditionally been a less developed market for venture capital as national differences in culture, accounting and company law have made it difficult for a deal-stream to develop. However, with the gradual deregulation of the markets in preparation for 1992, opportunities are opening up and joint ventures are being established between UK operators and European banks and institutions.

It is clear that the venture capital industry has become very well established during the last decade and has proved an attractive option for institutional investors. The industry has been a major contributor to the upsurge of corporate activity which has taken place during the period and has proved very successful in providing capital for the small to medium corporate entities. Financial techniques have become increasingly sophisticated and the range of possible financing structures has never been wider, particularly with the growth in mezzanine finance in the United Kingdom. The future of the industry is likely to see the development of several tiers of venture capitalists, as the larger groups specialise in giant MBOs and MBIs and the smaller develop niche specialities which enable them to generate good returns. In this way the industry is likely to maintain an across the waterfront service as a whole, from seed capital to the larger billion pound deals.

PART THREE

RESOURCE MANAGEMENT

12

❧

INVESTMENT MANAGEMENT

BRIAN D. WOOD

Extended growth and significant change have been keynotes of the recent development of investment management as the lengthy bull market in equities during the 1980s gave existing investment management firms a period of sustained expansion and led to a sharp increase in competition, both domestic and foreign. The concurrent structural changes in the UK investment market and the introduction of a new regulatory environment have been equally important in the transformation of the investment business. The investment divisions of the merchant banks have played leading roles and, despite the internationalisation of business and the appearance of domestic competition, continue to occupy a strong position in the market.

The merchant banks' involvement in investment management activities stems from a combination of historic accident and a traditional ability to adapt available skills to a constantly changing environment. It genesis lay in the development of large fortunes made by Victorian merchant banks, and developed through the requirement to handle the investments of their trading clients and moneyed friends. Their first major experience of handling public funds was the short-lived investment trust boom of the late 1920s.

Until the 1950s, the techniques of investment management were unsophisticated and relied upon long-accepted rules of investment based on the soundness of fixed-interest securities, particularly government stocks. Few merchant banks had many specialist investment staff or, indeed, a specific investment division. Portfolios were often in the care of partners or directors who had many other banking or corporate responsibilities.

By the mid 1950s, a number of important social and economic developments had taken place. Perhaps the most significant was that inflation had secured a firm foothold, although at low rates. At the same time, the sources of savings and capital had become much more widely spread and savings were beginning to move from the traditional havens of savings banks and building societies into the more inflation-proofed unit trusts and with-profits life policies.

Pension Fund investment

The number and coverage of pension funds, once the prerogative of the Civil Service, white-collar staff and the professions, grew rapidly with the collective responsibility philosophy of the post-war Welfare State and the provisions of the Taxes Acts allowing superannuation contributions to accumulate free of tax.

The merchant banks reacted quickly to the considerable increase in the flow of capital. They built on their existing skills and knowledge to deal efficiently with the increased volume of capital and with the greater complexity of the financial and political world, which has made investment judgement more and more difficult.

As time, taxation and social change took toll of large personal fortunes, the importance of private portfolio management to merchant banks diminished, making way for management of newer forms of capital aggregation, such as investment trusts and unit trusts.

An event of considerable developmental importance was the October 1986 stock-market Big Bang, which affected investment management firms as much as the stockbrokers and jobbers which were the primary target of the reorganisation. The abolition of stamp duty and minimum commissions on equity transactions led to a significant reduction in pension fund costs, leading to a surge in equity turnover. Pension funds have much less inhibition about switching equity holdings than other investing institutions, and this is a factor which must be taken into account in considering the allegations of short-termism which have been levelled at fund managers.

The traditional mainstay of the UK investment management firm, institutional pension fund management, has itself been through a period of significant growth in the 1980s. The total value of UK pension fund assets increased from £40 billion in 1979 to £200 billion in 1987 as markets provided several years of real returns significantly in excess of actuarial assumptions. Investment fees, which are linked to the value of assets under management, increased in line and the recognition of pension fund management as a highly profitable business attracted a host of new competitors, from international investment houses to domestic boutiques doing nothing but this activity.

In this environment, the investment divisions of the merchant banks, which had traditionally picked up business primarily through corporate contacts, found that for the first time they had to market themselves actively. The performance record of returns on existing investments is now of greater importance than the traditional emphasis on good name and contacts as the market has transformed from being a quasi-cartel to becoming one of the most competitive in the financial services industry.

Several other developments have gone hand-in-hand with the more intense competition. First, better performance and service. It is now customary for trustees of a UK pension fund to receive quarterly figures for the return on assets managed by any one firm, with further details of the return achieved in each of the main asset categories, as well as an estimate of the ranking of such returns compared with other fund managers. Such figures are closely scrutinised by the trustees and their consultants, and a string of poor quarterly results is likely to lead to the manager's dismissal.

This development has been blamed for the so-called herd instinct, where managers are reluctant to depart from average asset allocations for fear of underperformance. Some commentators even sought to blame performance measurement for the October 1987 stock market crash, on the grounds that managers were unwilling to take a long-term view and disinvest from an overvalued equity sector until they all did. Representatives of industry have also criticised excessive 'short-termism' among fund managers, whom they see as increasingly fickle shareholders, willing to take the money and run in take-over bids for the sake of profit and return, rather than take a long-term view of the pros and cons of the takeover approach. The arguments on both sides of this debate are complicated, but performance measurement is here to stay. The events of October 1987 put the chase for short-term gain into perspective, and the debate may subside if trustees are willing to agree long-term strategies with their investment managers.

Indexation

Another direct result of the growth and increasing sophistication of performance measurement has been the discovery, well publicised by pension fund consultants, that over the long term the majority of UK equity portfolios entrusted to active managers have underperformed the return on a representative index of constituent stocks. This realisation, together with the development of sophisticated computer-based stock selection systems, has been the main impulse for the development of index-tracking funds. These have gained increasing acceptance in the United Kingdom, following US experience.

Many naïve and often fallacious arguments have been adduced in favour of indexation. It is to be expected that the average actively-managed UK equity fund should produce a return slightly below that of the market index over the long term, once investment and dealing costs are taken into account, as the index return will obviously not suffer such deductions. It is, however, wrong to imply that the underperformance of the average fund over the long term discredits active management in general. Many investment houses have produced long-term returns in excess of the indices of the markets in which they invest, whilst others have underperformed.

Index-tracking funds usually only 'track' the index to within half a percentage point. But, despite their conceptual unattractiveness to some fund managers, they are likely to form a stable proportion of total managed funds, with attractions for those investors seeking standard returns at low cost. And they can be seen as the most accurate benchmark against which to judge the performance of the active manager.

Specialist managers

In addition to indexation, many pension fund consultants have been promoting a range of specialist investment services, in contrast to the balanced service traditionally offered by investment firms and in particular the merchant banks. Under the balanced approach, all assets are ceded to the investment manager, who allocates a proportion to different investment markets and manages them all in-house. The specialist approach envisages an overall asset allocator delegating assets to managers with good records in stock selection for various respective markets, quite possibly with a core of assets invested in an index-matching UK equity fund. Although conceptually neat, the specialist approach generally costs more than the balanced approach, and several investment managers have questioned moves to delegate asset allocation to a consultant with no investment experience, using a quantitative model to allocate assets on the basis of extrapolated past returns.

Independent firms offering specialist services have made inroads into the pension fund market at the expense of the merchant banks, although members of the former Accepting Houses Committee maintain a large overall share. Overall, however, the debate on the types and quality of pension fund management should prove beneficial to users of such services – the pension fund and, ultimately, members of such funds.

International investment

The main barrier to overseas investment by pension funds was lifted by the suspension of exchange controls in October 1979, and their subsequent abolition. The average proportion of pension fund assets invested in overseas equity markets rose from 3 percent in 1979 to 20 percent ten years later. The total proportion invested overseas is effectively higher than this, since around 35 percent of the profits of UK companies are derived from overseas subsidiaries.

The main motivations for overseas investment by pension funds have been to achieve superior returns and to reduce portfolio volatility by diversification. The Labour party has stated a desire to reduce the level of overseas investment, but while the political climate prevailing in the 1980s continues the proportion of overseas assets held by pension funds is likely to be maintained and perhaps increased. There is an obvious link between this proportion, the growing rate of corporate cross-border investment and the increase in world trade.

Merchant banks, with their long history of involvement in overseas trade and investment, have been major beneficiaries of this trend. Many have maintained a network of international offices, which have been put to good use in providing local knowledge essential to improve returns on overseas portfolios. However, the average performance of UK fund managers in overseas equity markets has been unspectacular, increasing the pressure to hire native managers for overseas markets and/or to invest in index-tracking funds.

A parallel trend from which many merchant banks have prospered has been the increase in overseas investment by the huge American pension fund market. The volume of assets in funds set up under the 1974 Employee Retirement Income Security Act, or ERISA, rose from $7 billion at the end of 1982 to $55 billion within six years. Many merchant banks have set up subsidiary operations to cater directly for this market, and have had considerable success in winning mandates. There is still room for considerable growth in this market.

But despite the growth in world trade, there are still limits on overseas investment in many countries, and there is great competition for existing management roles by established international investment houses. Nevertheless, the strong international links of the UK merchant banks are likely to offer continued scope in this field.

Other services

Merchant banks offer a number of other investment management services and vehicles, including unit trusts, offshore funds, property investment, venture capital and private client portfolio management.

The unit trust market is expected to grow in significance. This is due to moves by the Government to encourage the growth of personal pensions at the expense of the traditional institutional pension fund which was felt to restrict choice of benefit arrangements by employees and discourage labour mobility. Although tax incentives have been granted to encourage employees to set up personal pension policies, there was initially no significant shift away from institutional schemes, many of which continued to offer competitive benefits packages. Nevertheless, personal pensions have the potential to grow considerably and many merchant banks have positioned themselves to take advantage of this.

Structural changes in investment markets

The changes in the legal and regulatory framework which took effect in the late 1980s had far-reaching effects on investment managers' relations with clients. Before Big Bang in 1986, fund managers had charged clients standard commission rates to all clients on deals over a certain period, whilst taking the benefit of aggregating share purchases or sales on behalf of several clients, where lower commission rates were charged. After Big Bang this practice, known as aggregation, disappeared. Managers had to revert to charging directly, often raising fee scales as a result. Whilst the trend towards more transparent charging is generally to be welcomed, it has caused problems as some clients preferred indirect forms of payment when it was politically difficult to raise direct fees. Nevertheless, London remains the world's cheapest centre for investment management.

It was recognised at the time of Big Bang that there were real potential conflicts of interest between the investment management arm of a financial conglomerate and other divisions, notably those concerned with securities dealing and corporate finance. Many merchant banks have effectively become conglomerates, so to avoid such conflicts the investment management divisions were frequently separated physically from the rest. Indeed, in 1987 S.G. Warburg Group floated its investment arm as Mercury Asset Management. But the biggest constraint on breaches of confidence has been the sheer scale of damage it would inflict on an organisation's reputation among its clients and the investment community at large.

The regulatory environment

The 1986 Financial Services Act had consequences for investment managers as significant as Big Bang, if not more so. A completely new regulatory structure was evolved in the wake of the Act, enshrining in law many rules which had traditionally been considered 'best practice' by the merchant banks.

The Investment Management Regulatory Organisation (IMRO) was formed to supervise the investment management sector. To do so it had to provide a detailed code of practice for its members, which include all investment management firms. Without IMRO authorisation they cannot do business.

It will not be until the turn of the century that we shall be able to make a considered judgement of the effect of the new regulatory environment on the fundamentally entrepreneurial approach of the merchant banking community to investment activities. Conformity is the watchword of the Financial Services Act, and merchant banks have historically thrived on not conforming, taking unpredictable initiatives to capitalise on opportunities as they have presented themselves. This is of course not to say that merchant banking investment departments will not adhere to legal requirements, but as they become separated from their parents' other operations by Chinese walls and other devices, they may lose some of that uniquely pragmatic flavour which has marked them out from their peers.

13

MONEY-BROKING

E. C. PANK

What is a money-broker?

A broker is an intermediary who facilitates a transaction between two principals. A dealer is a principal who buys and sells for his own account. Money-brokers act as intermediaries between dealers in the deposit and foreign exchange markets. The business can be divided into three main activities as follows:

1. Foreign exchange broking.
2. Deposit broking.
3. The broking of off-balance sheet instruments.

The money-broker's profit as a commission agent depends on the volume of trades in which he intermediates and volatility of exchange and interest rates increases volume. The broker aims to provide the ideal market-place with good, accurate communications, high speed execution, and confidentiality. The customer can then make his assessment of the market and decide how to deal, and is most likely to place his business through an efficient provider of information and execution. Brokerage is calculated in the principal currency of the transaction in deposit markets, while in the foreign exchange market all London customers are charged in sterling, regardless of the currency dealt in, and some European customers are charged in Deutschmarks or Swiss francs, again regardless of the currencies involved in the actual transaction.

The major customers in all markets are the large international banks. Increasingly, however, corporate treasurers are using the services of money-brokers direct, although this is still a very minor part of the market. The service provided by the money-broker gives the banks and other customers access to the best prices in markets where significant price changes can take place in seconds. The money-broker is neutral in the market, merely quoting customer's prices. Therefore, unlike other markets where a market-maker in the middle is running his own book, there is no jobber's turn in the money-markets and the prices on each side of a deal match exactly. The broker's interest is only in transacting the largest possible volume of business. The provision of fast, accurate, up-to-date price information together with real trading propositions and the capability to execute them is the core of the money-broker's role. The money-broker potentially has access to all the price information in the world.

The major brokers have lines to all the major banks in the world. Usually these are direct open lines for which a fixed rent is paid. Increasingly modern technology is used, such as a digital feed through international fibre optic cables which more and more are replacing satellites because of increased speed of transmission and reliability. RLX can connect up to eight voice lines using a small portion of the overall bandwidth available in the fibre optic cable.

The broker's desk may have between 60 and 240 lines, each labelled for a particular bank or other customer, and swift response and passage of information and transmission of firm propositions gets business done. Speed of transmission of information and prices is vital. It would take a customer a very long time to telephone a comparable number of market counterparties. The service also provides a degree of anonymity, as no market participant knows of the positions of any other market participant because names are passed by the broker only when a deal is agreed.

Money-broking is mainly concentrated in the major financial centres of the world: New York, Tokyo and London. Whilst money-broking was well established in the United States and United Kingdom between the world wars, it was not established in Japan until the early 1970s. The other commercial centres of the world all have substantial international money-broking as well as purely domestic operations which have good access to the larger markets, as this is entirely a telephone market. The market effectively moves round the world with the sun. With three major centres, each becomes the centre of the market in turn and the prices at which each centre opens for business are based on those passed on by the market which is in the process of closing down. These opening prices will be adjusted by the view taken by the market that is opening and with longer office hours world-wide the overlap between markets is increasing. The major currencies traded are US dollars, Japanese yen, Deutschmarks, sterling and Swiss francs. Minor currencies are known as 'exotics'.

The business cycles operating in each part of the world may be different but they are interdependent. The different interest rates prevailing in different currencies are in part an arbitrage of future exchange rates as well as being instruments of government policy, and they are also short-term responses to economic news.

The speed of information flow now irons out anomalies very quickly, so that arbitrage opportunities between exchange rate risks and interest rates exist for very short periods of time, making the rapid delivery of accurate prices by brokers to dealers very valuable indeed. This is so whether a dealer is engaged in trading as an independently profitable activity on behalf of his employing bank, portfolio management, effecting a transaction in response to an underlying commercial need for a customer or hedging his position to limit the risk in any one of these activities.

As exchange rates and interest rates often move in response to each other, interest rates on deposits and foreign exchange rates often show movement at the same time. Fashions can be seen in currencies and off-balance sheet instruments. Major movements are increasingly seen in response to the announcement of financial statistics, especially those from the United States. Brokers and dealers will be awaiting the announcement of (for instance) the monthly trade deficit of the United States. There will be a consensus as to what figure is expected and when the figure appears simultaneously on the screens of all market participants, there can be a surge of activity in the markets in response, especially to statistics out of line with market expectations. Generally the greater the discrepancy from market expectations, the greater the volume of activity generated.

It is probable that perhaps 60 percent of the foreign exchange business in London is conducted directly between banks, especially where arrangements exist between banks to accommodate each other up to an amount of say £20 million, leaving 40 percent to be conducted through brokers. The Bank of England survey of March 1986 found that 89 percent of the London foreign exchange market was interbank, with 43 percent conducted through brokers. Money-brokers may be responsible for the smaller transactions in the market.

The money-broker is a 'name passing' broker. Customers of course know the size and rate of the deal when it is agreed. They may know the nationality and approximate size of the institution with whom they are about to deal, but the exact identity is revealed only after the deal is agreed and the parties are each passed the name of their counterparty.

It is impossible for dealers to form any clear idea of what positions other market participants may be wishing to take or unwind. Before Midland Bank made an announcement in January 1985 of the reorganisation of Crocker National Bank, the Midland dealers transferred Midland's market position from borrowings of £2 billion to a cash holding of £2 billion in the space of 30 days. This £4 billion turnaround went undetected in the money-markets, the market participants being unaware of the existence, let alone the scale, of the operation. Midland was of course careful to pay only market rates.

This transaction also bears witness to the liquidity of the markets. The survey conducted by the Bank of England in March 1986 estimated volumes in the foreign exchange markets in London to be equivalent to US$115 billion per day. Of this it is thought that only a small part is required to finance world trade. The rest represents changes in investment decisions by institutions, the covering of investments, and speculation. A further such survey has been carried out in April 1989 and the findings of the survey are expected to be published.

Names are passed only when the deal is done, but a general description such as 'large Japanese' or 'Clearer' is given. Market participants' positions are taken and unwound with such rapidity that no participant has an accurate picture of market positions at any one time.

In all the major centres, the prices quoted by money-brokers are 'firm', thereby greatly improving the service offered to banks. Where he quotes firm prices, always subject to acceptability of names, the money-broker is committed to procuring the other part of the transaction, subject to the counterparties having available limits with each other. A proposition is said to be 'under reference' where prerequisites such as the requirement for an off-setting transaction exist. Firm prices considerably increase market liquidity, and therefore volumes, and they therefore probably increase volatility also.

Foreign exchange broking

The original money-broking business was foreign exchange broking. Dealing in foreign exchange was already an old business when the money-changers were thrown out of the Temple in Jerusalem about 2000 years ago. For most of the last century the major foreign exchange markets were in Amsterdam, Berlin and Vienna. The need for a foreign exchange market in London was curtailed by the fact that much of the world trade was invoiced and financed in sterling. Foreign exchange broking started towards the end of the last century. Between the world wars there was a large number of small foreign exchange brokers in London. When the market re-opened in 1951, after having been closed down at the opening of hostilities in 1939, there were eight brokers who formed the Foreign Exchange Brokers Association, which has now enlarged its membership and become the Foreign Exchange and Currency Deposit Brokers Association (FECDBA). Most major London foreign exchange brokers are members of the FECDBA, but membership is not compulsory.

Foreign exchange broking divides into spot and forward markets. Spot transactions are for 'immediate delivery', which in foreign exchange means two business days ahead. All other transactions are forward transactions. The delivery or payment date is always referred to as the 'value' date. The spot markets are larger volume, probably providing three-quarters of commission for foreign exchange brokers, and are more volatile.

In the spot markets brokers quote actual prices all the time. Many brokers now conduct spot business through open lines to the banks where the rate is shouted out through a speaker. The banks can hear all the prices quoted by the brokers but the brokers cannot hear conversations at the bank's end. The prices are firm for delivery in two days' time and banks may 'hit' the price at any time, thereby instantaneously concluding a firm contract through the broker, who matches the trades subject only to the names being mutually acceptable and to credit limits. The term 'switch' normally refers to the process where a mutually acceptable name is put between two mutually unacceptable names, such as Arab and Israeli Banks. Where names are not acceptable, the broker will 'switch' the trade using an acceptable name as an intermediary.

Of their nature the forward foreign exchange markets are slower moving and they are probably diminishing in volume at the present time. Six months is the commonest contract in forwards with the one and three month contracts also common.

Forward contracts may be used to roll short positions over or by a borrower in a currency to cover repayment in that currency. The attraction of forward trading as a speculative activity is diminished, because to be successful dealing requires accurate prediction of the interest rates of the two currencies prevailing until the transaction is closed, as well as their relative exchange rates at that time specified for delivery in the contract. Further, it does involve a more substantial credit risk between the counterparties which again detracts. In the forward markets the banks' credit limits are especially important. If a bank's credit lines are full the name introduced by the broker will be refused and the broker will try to find another which is acceptable to complete the transaction.

Foreign exchange world-wide is organised on the basis that all currencies are traded against the US dollar. Historically this can be traced to the Bretton Woods conference, as a result of which all the principal currencies had a fixed value against the US dollar, which was itself convertible into gold. The trading of any currency against a currency other than the US dollar is called cross-currency trading. Cross-currency trading is mainly in the spot market and it consists mainly of the trading of other currencies against the Deutschmark. The major cross-currency markets are mark/yen, sterling/mark and mark/Swiss franc. Since the European Monetary System ties the small European currencies to the Deutschmark and US dollar/Deutschmark is the largest market world-wide in foreign exchange, it was natural that the cross-currency markets should develop in this way. In the United Kingdom, spot US dollar/sterling is the major foreign exchange market. It is known in the business as 'Cable' because settlement was originally be telegraphic transfer, rather than mail, which also introduced the two-day settlement in the spot foreign exchange markets.

New foreign exchange instruments such as the Exchange Rate Agreement (ERA) and the Forward Exchange Agreement (FXA) have recently been introduced. These are discussed below under off-balance sheet instruments.

Deposit-Broking

The next money-broking business to develop was deposit-broking, which gathered pace in the early 1960s. Deposit-broking is a business which facilitates the rearrangement of banks' and institutions' asset portfolios. As deposit-broking, like foreign exchange broking, is viewed as an independent profit centre by the banks and other participants, the emphasis is on currencies in which there is sufficient liquidity for large scale trading. Deposits in these currencies are there attractive assets for banks, other financial institutions and the treasurers of large corporations.

Sterling deposit-broking

Sterling deposit-broking in London is conducted as a separate business from Eurocurrency deposit-broking and is probably smaller in total volume in London than the London Eurodollar market. However, the customer base is broader than the other London markets. The Bank of England uses the market to influence rates through the discount houses, while building societies, UK county and municipal councils, and corporate customers all use the market as well as the banks. The main centre of the sterling deposit market is London. The Japanese are the most active participants outside the United Kingdom and Channel Islands' brokers are also active in the market.

Any maturity date for an odd number of days can be accommodated in this market. For the banks, less than one month is a short date, one month to one year is normal and over one year is a long date.

The recent movement from the cash markets to off-balance sheet instruments has been gaining momentum in the sterling deposit market as capital requirements for London subsidiaries of overseas banks have increased. Interest rate swaps are important whilst Forward Rate Agreements (FRAs) which are truly a bet, are not far behind. The downside is known, namely the loss of the commission paid to purchase the option. The international moves to standardise the calculation of capital for banks recommended by the Cooke Report are expected to make these off-balance sheet instruments less attractive to banks, as they are now in whole or in part being brought into the balance sheet calculations. Balance sheets may be restructured as a result.

In the sterling deposit market as in others, banks deal subject to credit limits which typically would be 10 percent of capital and reserves of the counterparty. All London sterling deposit-brokers are members of the Sterling Brokers Association which acts as a forum for exchange of views and the discussion of mutual problems including administrative matters.

The Eurodollar deposit market

Globally, the Eurodollar deposit market is the largest, driven by the money supply of the United States. The worsening deficit in the United States directly fuels the Eurodollar market. The dollar probably constitutes 45 percent of the non-sterling deposit market in London with the Deutschmark constituting 25 percent and the yen 20 percent, while all other currencies constitute 10 percent.

In the Eurodollar deposit market short deposits are up to twenty-eight days maturity, term is up to two years, two to five years is medium term with five-year maturity still fairly liquid. For maturities over five years the market is mainly in swaps. In the longer maturities, bonds are alternatives. US Treasury bills are possibilities for maturities of less than five years. Credit limits are important in this market, and this is also true in the short dates where an earlier payment date focuses attention on this aspect.

The first Eurocurrency off-balance sheet instruments were futures. This is a huge market and is mainly conducted by US banks rather than money-brokers now. Interest rate swaps are favoured because they take away physical lending and borrowing, and paying and taking interest on the basis of nominal sums. Interest rates options are an attractive alternative to the banks. Caps and floors are further examples of contracts for differences. Swaptions and currency options are significant. Most Eurocurrency deposit brokers are members of Foreign Exchange and Currency Deposit Brokers Association.

Off-balance sheet instruments

Off-balance sheet products are usually developed in response to end-user needs, namely the needs of the corporate treasurers of the banks' large customers. The first off-balance sheet instrument to be developed was the futures contract, while swaps were next. Because of the low counterparty risk involved in the futures market, counterparties of low credit standing find this market very attractive and are able to transact business on the same terms as institutions of the highest creditworthiness.

The market in off-balance sheet instruments started to develop in the late 1970s and early 1980s and has subsequently developed into a diverse range of money-market instruments in which the volume of trading has come to equal, or exceed, the trading in the traditional cash-based instruments. The terms of and conditions of many of the off-balance sheets have been standardised in documentation issued by the British Bankers Association. This is also the case in the interest rate swap market, although much standardisation work in this market has taken place under the auspices of the International Swap Dealers Association.

The spur of the evolution of this market was the necessity for banks to increase the quality of their return on assets and their ratio of earnings in relation to their balance sheet footings. Concerns regarding credit exposure of banks in trading 'on-balance sheet' risk also fuelled the development of alternative methods of dealing. Several different off-balance sheet instruments evolved to cater for differing needs of the international bank dealing community and their customers, and some of these instruments in turn led to the development of other, second generation, off-balance sheet products.

The main off-balance sheet instruments that have become firmly established in the money-markets are financial futures, cross-currency and interest swaps, forward rate agreements, forward exchange agreements, exchange rate agreements, currency options and various interest rate option instruments such as caps and floors, interest rate guarantees and options on government bonds.

Apart from the option type of instrument, which may result in the delivery of other cash instruments and certain futures contracts, most of these instruments represent contracts for differences. The principal feature of these instruments is that when the deals are effected there is no movement of principal amounts (which remain purely notional) and therefore significantly diminished credit risk.

Financial futures were the first off-balance sheet instruments to evolve and were the result of applying the already established dealing format of commodity futures to financial instruments. The pioneering development occurred in the United States, which still has the greatest share of global financial futures activity. The fact that futures are traded on specialised exchanges backed by a clearing house and incorporating a daily cash margin system also ensures that as well as being off-balance sheet, trading in these instruments is virtually free of counterparty credit risk.

The fact that futures are traded on specialised exchanges means that these instruments have been taken outside the normal area of the money-broker who operates in a telephone market. The futures exchanges have their own trading floors and in London this is the London International Financial Futures Exchange (LIFFE). However, the other off-balance sheet instruments which have developed as a direct result of the growth of financial futures, such as the FRA, continue to be traded in a telephone market.

The FRA is an over-the-counter (or interbank) future where the transacting parties are in essence betting with one another on the future level of interest rates when settlement occurs with the losing party paying to the winning party a sum calculated on a notional principal amount of money on the difference between the quoted interest rate on dealing and the actual rate prevailing at the maturity of the FRA.

The credit risk in this type of transaction is transformed from a customer-credit risk into a market-related risk because, as no principal changes hands, the worst loss that can result is the cost of replacing the deal in the market at adverse rates should the counterparty default before the transaction is completed. The nature of this instrument means that large positions can be built up and unwound by banks in a short period of time, either for risk management or speculative purposes, and this encourages the existence of an active and liquid market in all the major currencies in London and other major financial centres. Money-brokers play a very active role in the FRA market and enhance the speed and liquidity of the market in this instrument.

The interest rate swap market originally came about largely as a facility for bartering of relative advantages between a variety of financial institutions in terms of the cost of credit in either the floating rate and fixed rate markets, and between institutions of different nationalities. Financial institutions that could raise money cheaply in the fixed-term market might seek to exchange that advantage with a less fortunate counterparty who nevertheless had access to floating rate funds, and enter into a transaction that would result in the first institution being able to produce significantly cheaper floating rate money.

The basis for the interest rate swap is an agreement to exchange at regular intervals (or swap) the fixed and the floating interest payments according to an agreed formula. As this market developed the banks became active participants and built up significant books or 'warehouses' in these swaps. Money-brokers intermediate between the banks, who are constantly needing to adjust their positions in line with their changing risk perceptions. Interest rate swaps also can be made to interact with other off-balance sheet instruments and can be used as vehicles for institutional speculation.

The ERA and FXA are foreign instruments that have been developed recently by two of the clearing banks (Barclays and Midland) to try to use the off-balance sheet concept to reduce the credit risk implications of trading in the forward foreign exchange market. They are similar to the FRA and work on the principal of payments for differences between counterparties rather than the exchange of principal amounts. The existence of similar but essentially competing instruments being developed and sponsored by different banks has slowed the development and general acceptance of this instrument. Both these instruments provide similar cover and the market is trying to develop a new 'synthetic' instrument encompassing the most desirable features of the FXA and ERA. FXAs and ERAs are now governed by the British Bankers' Association document of April 1989 entitled *Synthetic Agreements for Foreign Exchange* and they are accordingly known collectively as SAFEs.

The most recent class of off-balance sheet instrument to develop in the money-markets (with the exception of the ERA and FXA) is that of options. Options have developed on a range of money-market instruments but the most successful to date are currency options.

Foreign exchange rates, since the abandonment of the Bretton Woods convention, have become increasingly volatile and this has been a major spur to the use of options on currencies to either speculate in or hedge against significant daily movements in the major world currencies. The large daily throughput of transactions in the spot market is another factor and options can be an attractive medium for obtaining significant extra leverage in the foreign exchange market. A large number of banks now trade in currency options actively in most of the world's major financial centres. Money-brokers serving this market need to have sophisticated personal computer support to enable them to calculate option prices for their customers on a wide range of currencies and to be able to quote for any combination of strike price and option expiry. Speed of communication and access to the fast-moving foreign exchange market are also attributes that the money-broker provides to customers in this market.

Of the various interest rate option instruments that have developed, the interest rate guarantee is effectively an option on a FRA which offers additional flexibility to institutions seeking to structure their exposure to short-term interest rate risk. Over-the-counter options are available on most of the actively traded Government bonds and provide an alternative to the bond option contracts offered on various futures exchanges. Interest rate caps and floors are mechanisms whereby institutions can obtain an instrument for controlling exposure to floating rate risk over a period of up to ten years. This is again essentially a contract for differences whereby the buyer of the option will receive from the seller a payment if the floating rate is higher (in the case of a cap) or lower (in the case of a floor) than the strike price of the option at each reset of the floating rate over the life of the option. The payment will be calculated on the agreed nominal amount by reference to the difference between the strike price and the actual floating rate at the time of reset.

As many of these newer instruments are complex, it is necessary for the money-broker to be able to provide an expert and technically competent service requiring both experienced and technically knowledgeable staff, together with sophisticated computer and telecoms systems.

Many of the off-balance sheet instruments can be used either in combination with each other or with cash-type instruments to create 'arbitrage' deals. Monitoring and execution of these transactions is another service which a money-broker offers to its customers.

Whilst the effect of the Cooke Report's recommendations to give greater capital weighting to off-balance sheet instruments has made these instruments less attractive to banks, the effect on the market has been diminished as the weighting is still less than the 100 percent weighting for the actual obligation and therefore they are still to be preferred to the actual product.

Regulation

In the United Kingdom money-brokers are regulated by the Bank of England's Wholesale Markets Supervision Division. To broke investment instruments in the United Kingdom, money-brokers have to be listed by the Bank of England under Section 43 of the Financial Services Act 1986 (unless authorised by a self-regulating organisation). When listed by the Bank of England they are then exempt from the provisions of the Financial Services Act but they are subject to the Bank's London Code of Conduct or 'Grey Paper' regime. As well as codifying existing rules of good practice the regime sets out the capital requirements for money-brokers. As name passing money-brokers do not have position risks, the normal requirement is the greater of £250,000 or two months' expenses. If the expenses figure submitted is not of sufficiently high quality, then a turnover requirement may be imposed.

There is an increasing movement towards 'convergence' or uniformity of regulations between countries. Close liaison is maintained between the Federal Reserve Banks in New York and Washington, the Bank of Japan and the Bank of England as well as with the Central Banks of the European Community, Canada and Australia, but it is not as advanced as in the field of banking.

The future

Technological developments will undoubtedly improve the mechanisms by which money-broking is carried out in the future. The past 20 years have seen a change from mechanical calculators and dealing rooms of half a dozen brokers to electronic screen information and sometimes as many as one hundred brokers in one room. These are moves towards a perfect market in the conceptual sense.

Under the Bretton Woods system of fixed-exchange rates, market volatility was miniscule compared with the violent swings of the modern market-place and yet, to the amazement of modern market participants, they still made money.

As the world becomes ever more international and the several market-places are increasingly replaced by one global market-place, the need for brokers to disseminate fast, accurate price information to produce an efficient and liquid market-place remains. The only certainty is that the service being offered by money-brokers will have changed in emphasis and also technology by the end of the millenium.

14

❦

BULLION DEALING

PETER HAMBRO

Introduction

Bullion dealing is all that remains of the merchant business from which the epithet 'Merchant Banking' derives. Many of the great banking houses of Europe have origins in the business of buying, selling and storing goods of one sort or another – Hambros and Rothschilds are classic examples – and it was only the excellent reputation that they earned in this activity which allowed them to add creditworthiness to the obligations of their customers. This took them into the field of pure banking and only in a few cases do the vestigial traces of their past remain, in the form of bullion dealing. Of those banks commonly thought of as merchant banks, N.M. Rothschild & Son, Samuel Montagu & Co. Ltd and Kleinwort Benson Ltd (through their ownership of Sharps Pixley) are the only ones which truly deserve the name; the others more correctly being described as accepting houses, or investment banks in the American idiom.

The dual nature of precious metals, and more particularly of gold, as both commodity and money is the principal reason that the business survives, backed by six thousand years of collective inherited memory of gold as a store of value and medium of exchange and the fact that for centuries purities of 995 parts per thousand have been within the reach of contemporary technology from a creation and verification.

Essentially the business has not changed from that of the Lombard financiers of the Middle Ages, or of the merchants of Hamburg or Frankfurt in the eighteenth century. It consists of exploiting the potential for arbitrage between commodity and money, given differences in delivery dates, locations and qualities. Being a member of the market-place involves quoting firm buying and selling prices for conventional amounts and delivery dates. Providing a service to the customers adds the need for more specialised activities. Depending on the nature of the house, there is also the possibility of attempting to profit from taking outright positions based on the view of the likely future course of prices.

Today the trading mechanism has much in common with the interbank

market in foreign exchange: trading by telephone, telex and Reuter Dealing
System rather than a defined market-place and time, and settlement of
interdealer transactions by means of accounting entries. Even the financial
futures aspect of modern foreign exchange is mirrored by the highly liquid
futures contracts on gold and silver on COMEX and on platinum on NYMEX
in New York. However, observers would be wise not to believe that the
businesses of foreign exchange and bullion trading are identical. Incaution
and inexperience in the complicated differences of the physical metals
markets can lead to problems which could not arise in the currency market.

Market Conventions

Wherever, however and whenever gold and silver are traded, the London
market is likely to be directly affected, for the majority of the world's gold and
silver are traded on the basis of 'Loco London'. This means that the price is
for a Troy ounce of metal in a bar of specific weight and purity tolerances
produced by a refiner on a list of acceptable melters, refiners and assayers
published by the London Bullion Market Association (LBMA). The bar must
also be held in one of the vaults operated by members of the LBMA.
Depending on the particular transaction, delivery may take place in some far
distant place and the metal may only be in a semi-refined state, or it may be of
extra high purity and in a hard-to-make shape. In such cases the price will be
quoted as a discount or premium to the Loco London price, depending on the
costs of refining, insurance, transport and carrying. Details of the specific
criteria for Loco London are contained in a brochure published by the
LBMA, but for convenience some of the technical aspects are reproduced in
Table 14.1.

Table 14.1. Good delivery specification for gold and silver bars

	Gold	Silver
Weight		
Maximum	350 fto	1250 Tr oz
Minimum	430 fto	500 Tr oz
Fineness	995/1000	999/1000
Marks	● Serial number ● Stamp of acceptable melter and assayer ● Fineness	● Serial number ● Stamp of acceptable melter and assayer ● Fineness ● Weight
Appearance	Bars should be of good appearance, free from cavities or other irregularities, layering and excessive shrinkage, and must be easy to handle and convenient to stack.	Bars should be of regular size for each of stacking and handling. The surfaces of bars should be free from layering, excessive shrinkage, cavities and other irregularities. The edges should be round and not sharp.

Tr oz = Troy ounce

Market-makers quote interdealer trading prices for 4,000 ounces of gold, 50,000 ounces of silver and 500 ounces of platinum against US dollars. Both are for 'spot' settlement (two London and/or New York banking days later). Metal is settled over 'Exchange Accounts', accounts maintained by the clearing members of the LBMA which represent Troy ounces (to three decimal places) of unallocated metal in their vaults. Money payments are by interbank transfer between banks in New York. Exceptionally, given the time difference between metal and money transfer, and the fact that very large sums change hands in this market, arrangements need to be made whereby the risk of settlement failure by one party can be eliminated.

By agreement, dealers will also quote for forward delivery. This enables both dealers and customers not only to match specific requirements, such as production schedules for example, but also to use simultaneous purchases and sales (swaps) as an alternative to money-market transactions. A central bank-holder of gold may conveniently and cheaply raise short-term finance by selling spot and buying back forward metal, in much the same way that Government Bond Repurchase Agreements are operated in London and New York. An active forward market also allows for switching between Loco London and the delivery dates on the futures markets. This means that dealers quote prices in 'Exchange for Physical' (EFP) where, for example COMEX futures contracts are exchanged at a premium for Loco London.

As in the foreign exchange market, contracts are made at the moment the deal is done, whether by telephone, telex or Reuter Dealing System. These are normally confirmed between dealers by telex as well as by mail confirmation and, as additional security against the risk of a deal getting lost in the system, many dealers will telephone each other to check out all the business done during a particular morning or afternoon.

The Fixings

Twice a day the members of the London Gold Fix, and daily the members of the London Silver Fix, meet to transact business at The Fixings. Much of the misconception which surrounds these events stems from the understanding of the word 'fix'. In this context it means 'determine', much as a sailor 'fixes', or determines his position in the middle of an ocean by means of a star sight. The market determines the world-wide price of the metal at a particular moment when all buyers and sellers are accommodated at a particular price. Because of the word's other meaning there are those who erroneously believe that the participants in some way arrange for the price to be set at some artificial level to suit the members' own ends. Not so.

The mechanism of the Fix is simplicity itself. The Chairman, the representative of Rothschilds in the case of gold and of Mocatta in the case of silver, chooses a price, approximately the one at which metal traded immediately before the Fix started, and announces it to the assembled representatives of the other members. They in their turn declare whether, at this price, they are buyers or sellers. In the event that there are both present, the chairman calls for figures – the amount of metal that buyers and sellers wish to transact at the price. If there is greater demand for metal than there is supply, he announces a new price, higher than the previous one, in the hope of tempting increased selling or curbing demand. If there is greater supply than demand he will do the opposite and lower the price. Only when supply and demand are matched will he declare the price fixed and at that level transactions between members take place. Very occasionally, and to bring a long and difficult fix to a speedy end, the chairman will declare the price fixed on a partial fill of buying and selling orders.

The system of fixing benefits a number of different interests in the market-place. These might be parties to long-term supply contracts who wish to have a bench-mark against which to measure their commitments, official holders who need to have open market valuations of metal in portfolio or large-scale buyers and sellers who need to be sure that the maximum possible number of potential participants are involved in the market at a particular moment to absorb the unusual quantity of business that they wish to transact. All find the system of great benefit.

Fixing members, since they cannot be definition profit from a dealing spread at the fixing, charge fixing commissions for handling the business.

Other markets

Although London's influence is very strong, there are active markets and local settlements of bullion elsewhere in the world. In the Far East, Hong Kong has dominated for some time but it is being challenged by Tokyo. Physical demand, particularly for gold, in Taiwan and Korea has reinforced the importance of these areas. Australian production has grown rapidly and the local market centred on Perth is of growing influence, as are Singapore and the jewellery industry in Bangkok. The Middle East, with the decline in oil revenues, has become less of a factor on its own account but, as a departure point for re-export to the thriving markets in India and Pakistan, the Gulf ports are very significant. In Europe, Zurich and Frankfurt are still the major competitors to London, with growing interest being shown by Paris. In North America the market is dominated by the futures contracts on COMEX and NYMEX but, with increased production from the area there is a growing demand for US and Canadian locations. In South America, a major producing continent, the market-places are relatively localised and the pricing is dominated by Loco London.

Risks

By its nature the trading of bullion involves risk. Apart from the risk of profit or loss arising from successful or unsuccessful speculation on price, there is the granting of credit. Although every effort will be made to ensure that counterparties are of good credit standing, there are occasions when this may not be sufficient.

Settlement

Settlement may be effected 'cash against delivery', in which case no risk should arise. In practice it is often the case that payment instructions have been given without evidence of delivery having been received, or vice versa. In certain cases this is inevitable owing to time differences between centres. In such cases it could occur that payment or delivery has already been effected when the counterparty defaults in settlement of his obligation. These risks must be monitored by effective delivery and settlement procedures.

Price fluctuation

Even in the case of a spot deal, two days normally elapse before settlement takes place. In the period between contract and settlement, prices may fluctuate adversely. After gold has been sold at a particular price on the contract date, the price may have weakened before the settlement date arrives. Should the counterparty default, the bullion dealer would need to 'close' the contract by selling at a loss to another counterparty. Such risks can be limited only by monitoring counterparties or by obtaining a sufficiently large deposit by way of margin before entering into the contract. Of course, further risks of loss arise in transport and delivery. In this respect, administrative procedures and insurance should exclude the risk of loss.

Administration

Positions

The monitoring and control of dealing positions is of utmost importance in limiting price risks. Prices can fluctuate rapidly, and substantial dealing can be achieved in a short period of time. It is essential that these control systems result in updated information at frequent intervals.

Limits

Based on credit analysis of counterparties and on past experience, limits should be established as to the volume and value of outstanding deals with any counterparty at any particular time. While the setting of such limits is the responsibility of management and the function of a credit department, limit administration normally takes place within the dealing room, so that prior to effecting a deal the existing risk exposure on a counterparty can be checked against his limit and confirmation received that a further deal will not cause the limit to be exceeded.

Margin administration

In the case of forward deals, or of spot deals which involve the extension of credit to the counterparty, bullion trading houses will often ask their counterparty to put up 'margin', consisting of cash or metal deposits or guarantees. Margin has two forms: an original margin on the initial contract, and a variation margin which is needed when the market price moves adversely in respect to the counterparty's position.

Delivery and Transport Procedures

This is a crucial area, and one with which the foreign exchange dealer would not be expected to be familiar. Conventional commodity trading companies have 'traffic departments' which handle all aspects of physical trading. In the case of the bullion house this will include, but not be limited to, negotiating insurance policies and premia, freight costs, refining charges, storage rentals and any other hidden extras which could turn overtly profitable business into losses. Some houses have shied away from this end of the business and tend to concentrate on the 'paper' trading aspects. Others treat it as a profit centre.

Unallocated and allocated storage

In the case of unallocated storage, counterparties who frequently deal with one another will, in most cases, avoid moving precious metals into specific vaults designated by the counterparty, but will use accounting entries to reflect their mutual bullion positions. To this end Nostro and Vostro accounts (similar to those used for cash relationships) are employed, in this case called 'Exchange Accounts', which are maintained in terms of ounces. Bullion dealers therefore owe and are owed precious metals which have not been specifically segregated in any vault and therefore constitute obligations similar to those of a bank, with the depositor being an unsecured general creditor in the event of a liquidation. This system of exchange accounts avoids the costly movement of precious metals and reduces administration.

In certain cases customers may require allocated storage of metal. Then it is physically segregated in a vault and the counterparty informed of the serial number, weight and fineness of bars allocated. The significance of allocated storage is that the bullion house acts as a custodian of the customer's property and the depositor's position in a liquidation is consequently improved. However, this type of storage involves handling, rental and insurance costs, and thus is not commonly used among professionals, except to spread credit risks prior to shipment. Other forms of storage of precious metals may also be evidenced by warrants, certificates and vault receipts.

Accounting

Bullion dealing involves specific accounting problems, especially so far as the valuation of future contracts is concerned. Valuation is necessary whenever profits require to be assessed. The sort of problem which arises can be easily illustrated by a forward arbitrage operation where several currencies are concerned. A dealer may have bought and sold metal for delivery on different dates in the future and for settlement in different currencies. To avoid an exchange risk he would have effected forward foreign exchange transactions for the sale of the currency he expects to receive, and for its conversion into the currency he will have to pay. Therefore, the valuation of metals positions will involve not only the forward metal positions themselves, but also foreign exchange positions and even loans and deposits.

Conclusion

Although steeped in history, bullion dealing is far from being an anachronism. The technological advances in recovery processes and improvements in geological survey and mining techniques have changed the face of the production side of the equation almost to the same extent that they have changed the face of Western Australia itself. Bullion dealers have responded to the challenge of these innovations by adapting their businesses to meet the needs of producers and finance houses. Gold loans, a technique long known in the jewellery finance business, have been adopted by a new breed of project-finance gold banker as a means of providing development capital for mines, and combination options, known as Price Protection Programmes, remove downside price risk in exchange for participation in possible upside profits, giving greater comfort to bankers lending money for the early stages of production.

The traditions of the merchant are alive and well in the hands of the bullion dealers, who still find both intellectual satisfaction and profit in their arcane world.

PART FOUR

SUPERVISION

15

❦

REGULATION UNDER THE
FINANCIAL SERVICES ACT

ROBIN DIX

Context

The regulatory regime for merchant banks, and indeed for other investment businesses, changed considerably in the spring of 1988, when the Financial Services Act 1986 came into force. The need for a new system of regulation had been recognised for some time, and was the more or less inevitable result of three developments.

First, during the 1970s and early 1980s a number of collapses and scandals in the investment world had pointed up gaps in the regulatory system then in force. That system had been based around the Prevention of Fraud (Investments) Act of 1958, but the regime did not, for example, cover dealing in commodity and other futures because at the time it was introduced there was no likelihood of any real public involvement in these markets. However, by the early 1980s it became clear that small investors could indeed be among the casualties when these firms went into liquidation. As they stood to lose their entire life savings in such a collapse, a High Court judge in 1983 warned small investors about the risks inherent in this form of investment and called on Parliament to establish safeguards.

The second reason for bringing in a new regime was the increased participation of private investors in financial markets. Commodity futures were by no means the only area where individuals, often with only a very limited knowledge of the products and the risks, now had a presence. An increasing number of people were entrusting money to financial advisers and managers, either for a personal portfolio management service or for pooled investments such as life insurance policies with a substantial investment element, or unit trusts. In other words, the trend towards increased participation by private investors in the financial services market predates by some years the Conservative Government's privatisation policies in the 1980s, although privatisation has been another contributory factor in that general trend

The third reason for introducing a new system of regulation was the need to adapt to changing conditions in the stock market. Particularly significant from a regulatory point of view was the abolition of minimum commissions and single capacity in 1986, and the consequent stimulus for a spate of mergers and takeovers (in many cases involving large financial institutions) among jobbers and brokers. This development greatly increased the number of possible conflicts of interest which a firm might face while carrying out a client's instructions. And the admission of foreign securities houses into London increased the number of large and unfamiliar players in the market.

The regulatory system introduced under the Financial Services Act is based on the recommendations of Professor Gower, who submitted a report on investor protection to the Government in 1984. His basic recommendation was that anyone conducting investment business in the United Kingdom should need authorisation in order to do so. Furthermore, he defined 'investment business' much more widely than before, including not only such areas as futures and options, but also long-term insurance contracts with an investment element, which had become very popular following the rise of the endowment mortgage.

Structure of the new regime

The power to authorise and regulate investment businesses was vested by the Act in the Secretary of State at the Department of Trade and Industry, but it was always envisaged that this power should be delegated. It was delegated to the Securities and Investments Board (SIB), which received its designation order in the middle of 1987. By this stage work on setting up the regulatory structure envisaged in the Act, and indeed the drafting of the SIB rule-book, was already well advanced. It was by any standards a massive undertaking, especially in view of the fact that because investment businesses of any kind could come to SIB for authorisation, the rule-book had to cover all aspects of investment business.

But it was never intended that large numbers of firms should receive their authorisation from SIB. The Act provides for SIB to delegate much of the responsibility for regulating and monitoring individual investment businesses to self-regulating organisations (SROs), and to recognised professional bodies (RPBs) such as the Institutes of Chartered Accountants and the Law Societies. The result is that SIB is responsible for setting standards within the system as a whole, for ensuring that SROs and RPBs have rule-books which provide investors with a level of protection equivalent to that enjoyed under the SIB rule-book, and for monitoring the recognised bodies themselves, together with the relatively small number of investment businesses which have decided to come to SIB for direct authorisation.

There are five SROs, each responsible for different areas of the financial services market. These are as follows:

1. *The Association of Futures Brokers and Dealers (AFBD)* authorises and

monitors firms which deal, arrange deals and advise on deals in futures, options and contracts for differences, and which manage portfolios of these types of investments.

2. *The Financial Intermediaries, Managers and Brokers Regulatory Association (FIMBRA)* authorises and monitors firms which advise on and arrange deals in life insurance and units in collective investment schemes, and which provide investment advisory and management services to retail customers.

3. *The Investment Management Regulatory Organisation (IMRO)* authorises and monitors firms which offer discretionary management services, which manage and operate collective investment schemes and in-house pension funds, give investment advice to institutional investors, or which act as trustees for unit trusts and pension funds.

4. *The Life Assurance and Unit Trust Regulatory Organisation (LAUTRO)* regulates insurance companies and friendly societies engaged in retail marketing of life insurance products, and operators of regulated collective investment schemes engaged in the retail marketing of units in those schemes.

5. *The Securities Association (TSA)* regulates firms which deal and arrange deals in shares, debentures, gilts, warrants, certificates representing securities, rights and interests in securities, and financial futures and options on securities and their derivatives, and on foreign currency. It also covers firms which advise corporate finance customers and arrange deals for them.

The RPBs are nine in number: there are the three Law Societies, the three Institutes of Chartered Accountants, the Chartered Association of Certified Accountants, the Insurance Brokers' Registration Council and the Institute of Actuaries. According to the Financial Services Act, professional firms can obtain their authorisation from these professional bodies provided that their business is not wholly or mainly investment business. In the vast majority of cases, such firms are well below the limit: a solicitor may from time to time advise a client on how to invest an inheritance but such investment business will usually be only a small part of the activities of a professional practice.

In addition to recognising the SROs and RPBs, SIB can also recognise under the Financial Services Act investment exchanges and clearing houses. In order to gain recognition, an investment exchange must satisfy SIB that it has adequate financial resources, adequate safeguards for investors (including either its own clearing arrangements, or else appropriate agreements with a recognised clearing house), adequate monitoring and enforcement procedures, arrangements for the investigation of complaints, and a willingness to promote and maintain high standards of integrity and fair dealing. Investments need not be traded on such exchanges, but where the transaction is 'off exchange' a number of more onerous rules apply, particularly in the case of private investors.

The rules

Only the one hundred or so firms authorised by SIB are directly affected by the SIB rule-book in its entirety (although certain chapters of it, such as the rules on cancellation and compensation, apply more generally). But all the regulatory bodies recognised under the Financial Services Act must offer investor protection equivalent to that in SIB's own rule-book. So in a very real way the SIB rule-book sets the standards for the system as a whole.

Partly because it has to set standards across the board, and partly because firms in all parts of the financial services market have the right to apply to SIB for authorisation, the SIB rule-book covers all the main forms of investment business included in the Financial Services Act. Any attempt to shorten and simplify this multi-volume work as far as is consistent with SIB's responsibilities is limited. For one thing, there must be detailed rules to cover the activities of firms with direct authorisation. It is, however, feasible to incorporate statements of principle as well, in order to clarify the objectives which the rules are designed to achieve, and in the revision SIB proposed that this be done.

It is easy, owing to the inevitable detail, to become bogged down in the specific requirements relating to, say, the rules on advertising an investment in futures. But it is very important not to think of the rule-book as a large collection of *non sequitur*: there is a coherent overall structure to the regulations, and it helps immensely in coming to terms with them if that structure is grasped at the outset.

An investor's money is protected by three connected sets of rules. First, there are the financial resources rules, which require that a company should have financial resources proportionate to the risks inherent in the business it undertakes. Firms are required to comply with these rules on a continuous basis, and to report regularly to the authorities, so that their compliance can be monitored.

Secondly, there are the clients' money regulations, which provide for money belonging to investors to be held in trust and kept in a separate, or segregated, account. This means that if a company does go into default despite the safeguards in the capital adequacy rules, any money belonging to clients can be returned direct to them, rather than being distributed to the general creditors of the company. And finally, if despite these precautions investors find that their money is improperly lost, there is a central compensation scheme from which private individuals can claim up to £48,000.

But there are many factors in investment business not directly related to financial resources and the custody of other people's money. Another section of the rule-book therefore deals with regulating a firm's conduct of business. This chapter covers activities from advertising and the behaviour of salesmen to in-house complaints procedures and record-keeping. Yet even in this mixed bag there are themes which give the chapter as a whole a real consistency of purpose and coherence. When investment advice is being given, there is a rule that advisers should 'know their customer'. The most appropriate product will differ from investor to investor, depending on personal circumstances, financial commitments, investment objectives, and so forth. The rule which places this requirement on advisers is supported by a suitability rule, to ensure that people are not advised to buy an investment which is inappropriate for them. And for unit trusts and life policies, there is a further rule that the adviser should give 'best advice' – that is, that he or she should not recommend the purchase of one product instead of another which would better suit the client.

Another set of conduct of business rules have been devised to ensure that the investor knows where he or she stands. What, for instance, is the relationship with the adviser? For this reason SIB introduced the concept of 'polarisation' in the field of life insurance and unit trusts. 'Polarisation' means that an investment adviser must be either independent, acting as the agent of the investor, and in his best interests, or 'tied' to a single company, and recommending only its products. Where the adviser is tied, it is a requirement of the rules that he must disclose to the investor the limitations under which he is operating.

Other necessary disclosures include the requirement to inform the investor how much he is being charged for the product or services he is buying; the requirement to ensure that the customer understands the nature of the risk he is taking; the requirement that when an investor is being sold an investment which is not readily realisable he should be told that it may be more difficult to sell than to buy; and the requirement that the relationship between a company and a private investor is set out in a customer agreement, detailing the charges which will be levied, the kinds of investment covered, circumstances under which the customer can be cold-called, and so forth. And where a firm faces a conflict of interest, it must disclose the fact to the investor unless it has arrangements (such as a Chinese wall) in place to ensure that no clients are adversely affected.

Advertising is another crucially important area of the rules. An advertisement is often an investor's first contact with the company to whom he is going to entrust money – and first impressions are important. Apart from obvious requirements, such as the need for an advertisement to be true and fair not only in respect of what it includes, but also in respect of anything it omits, there is also a rule requiring a firm to state the name of its regulator when advertising a specific investment. And in the case of a 'money-off-the-page' advertisement – that is, where the reader is invited to send a cheque without further consideration or advice – there are extra requirements to ensure that the investor has enough information to make a reasoned investment decision.

Each individual legal entity – for instance, each company in a group – has to be separately authorised to conduct investment business, and has to comply on a continuous basis with all the rules of its regulator.

Merchant banking groups today undertake a very wide range of investment activities, and within any one group there will usually be a number of companies operating with authorisation from several different SROs. In many cases, the group will be structured in such a way that securities and futures, for instance, will be looked after by different companies within the group. But there is one major area where dual membership is usually required: unit trust managers will normally join both IMRO (for the fund management side of their business) and LAUTRO (to cover retail marketing). IMRO disapplies its marketing rules where a member company is also a member of LAUTRO, so that regulatory overlap is minimised.

Perhaps the area where most care needs to be taken in the event of multiple membership is where a group is so structured that a single company within the group provides services to the others. For example, if the dealing services for an entire group are provided by a single company within that group, the company providing the service is likely to have to observe, amongst other things, the staff dealing rules of each SRO to which a company within the group belongs.

The way forward

Between 1985 and the end of April 1988 when the Financial Services Act came into force, great energy was needed to establish SIB and the other regulatory bodies, draw up policies and rule-books, assess the SRO and RPB rule-books for equivalence, and begin the processing of applications.

But numerous tasks and initiatives remain to be undertaken now that the system has come into force. Much hard work is going into building relations with overseas regulators. It is particularly important to do this with the regulators of foreign companies which are operating in the United Kingdom on a branch basis. A branch does not have capital of its own: its financial health is inseparable from that of the company of which it is a part. As it is often not feasible satisfactorily to regulate or monitor from the United Kingdom the capital adequacy of companies which are established abroad, SIB is in the process of agreeing arrangements with overseas regulators, whereby the foreign regulators will monitor the firm's capital adequacy against their own rules, and let SIB know if a problem arises, so that appropriate action can be taken to protect investors in Britain. But there are also other benefits from this policy: while such arrangements do not cover matters like international fraud or illegal cold-calling, the relationships which are developed with overseas regulators in the process of drawing up the agreements mean that in the event of these misdemeanours it is easier to co-operate quickly and effectively, and so put an end to the abuse in question.

European Community directives on investment business, developed in preparation for the Single European Market in 1992, fully involved the SIB in the discussions on the form these important pieces of Community legislation should take. These aim to allow competition in financial services throughout the Community, by enabling investment businesses to operate in any member state on the basis of authorisation by the state in which they are based (the 'home state regulator'). SIB strongly supports this approach. At the same time it will be seeking to ensure that a proper degree of regulation in such areas as financial resources, segregation of clients' money, and compensation for private investors is monitored and enforced by each of the home state regulators. These matters are covered by the proposed Investment Services Directive and Capital Adequacy Directive and they represent the immediate priorities. Conduct of business will for the foreseeable future be regulated by the host state as distinct from the home state regulator.

At the same time SIB reviewed its rule-book to make it more 'user-friendly'. The first version was produced under enormous time pressure, and the SIB now aimed to achieve a simplification – or perhaps it would be more accurate to say a distillation – of the original text. SIB's aim in doing this was not to reduce investor protection, but rather to reduce where possible the length and complexity of the present version of the rules. Everyone, whether investment business or investors, should benefit from such an exercise.

Further initiatives are under way concerning the disclosure of commissions, charges and expenses in relation to life policies and unit trusts. From the beginning of 1990, investors should be informed of the amount of commission that their independent adviser stands to receive if his recommendation is followed. There is also to be clearer disclosure of the following factors:

1   The status of those who are not independent but can sell only the products of one company or group;
2. The overall effect of the different charges applied to a life policy;
3. The expenses in the case of a with-profits policy;
4. Other aspects of the with-profits policy which will determine the ultimate outcome for the investor (such as the company's bonus policy).

Conclusion

By any standards this is a demanding programme. Nor is there any sign of abatement in the longer term. Financial services companies are highly innovative, and in an increasingly competitive, volatile and international market regulators will constantly have new products, new practices and other matters to take account of. There are a number of quite fundamental questions on the agenda for consideration after the above concerns have been dealt with.

Take the capital adequacy rules. The present rules lay down financial resources requirements for individual companies, which are monitored for compliance. But what if another company within the group develops financial problems? The trouble may affect the other group members, despite the fact that in isolation they are financially sound. Would it be prudent for regulators to consider introducing some form of 'consolidated supervision' in an attempt to assess the financial health of the group as a whole, in addition to requiring compliance by the individual investment companies within it?

There are questions surrounding the subject of disclosure. When a unit trust manager was responsible for paying a large number of the trust's costs out of his own periodic fee, there was an understandable tendency to concentrate on disclosures relating to that fee. Now, however, many of these costs can be charged direct to the trust, rather than being paid by the manager, and disclosure will need to evolve to reflect the new reality.

In the investment world, circumstances change very quickly. New investment vehicles are constantly being developed and old lines of demarcation being redrawn (as, for example, banks increase their participation in the investment markets, and building societies diversify their activities beyond the provision of mortgages). Regulators, if they are to be effective, must keep such changes under review, and be ready to adjust to new realities, while at the same time ensuring that no regulatory lacunae open up among the increasingly various products on offer.

These are just some of the issues which face regulators in the United Kingdom, and indeed across the world. As the system of regulation under the Financial Services Act becomes established, and as the investment markets become more inextricably interlinked and more international, the need for, and the benefits of, co-operation between regulators on a global scale will become increasingly apparent. Already some fora have been developed, where regulators can meet to discuss ideas and experiences. Valuable work has already been done; the next priority must be to make further progress towards the harmonisation of key areas in the various regimes operated by the different regulators. This will be crucial in the development of effective regulation and agreed minimum standards of investor protection across the world. If this end is achieved, life will not only become much more difficult for the small number of crooks who sully the reputation of the large majority of reputable financial services firms: markets across the world will be able to operate more efficiently and standards of service to customers (whether corporate or private) will improve. All this should lead to the development of an environment in which investors have greater confidence that they will be properly treated, and so will be prepared to trust investment businesses.

16

❧

REGULATION AND SUPERVISION
BY THE BANK OF ENGLAND

DR MAXIMILIAN HALL

Introduction

The Bank of England's role as prudential regulator of 'authorised institutions' derives from concerns to protect depositors and to preserve the stability of the UK banking industry. The former objective is enshrined within the Banking Act 1987, while the latter goal derives from the central banking function concerned with ensuring overall financial stability – the so-called systemic interest – so as to facilitate the achievement by the incumbent political administration of its broader macroeconomic goals.

As within any system of financial regulation, the present framework comprises a mix of statutory and non-statutory controls. The Bank's statutory responsibilities stem, in the main, from the provisions of the Banking Act 1987, although additional demands arise from the Financial Services Act 1986, involving the Bank in the formal regulation of the securities operations of authorised institutions. The non-statutory elements of regulation depend upon the acceptance by practitioners of the authority of the Bank as central bank. This authority, however, may increasingly be challenged as the financial market-place becomes more litigious and the prominence of the foreign bank contingent continues to grow. This may presage a yet more formalised regulatory regime but, for the time being, the Bank remains determined to retain the maximum degree of discretion for itself in the interpretation and implementation of its statutory powers, and to persevere with the non-statutory regulation of the 'wholesale' markets. Periodic interviews with bank managements will also remain at the core of the supervisory process, as an inspection-based system is felt to be too inflexible.

Authorisation procedures

As required by Schedule 3 of the Banking Act 1987, an institution has to fulfil minimum criteria before gaining Bank authorisation. A bank must conduct business in a 'prudent manner' and with 'integrity and skill'; directors, controllers and managers must be 'fit and proper' persons; the bank has to have minimum net assets of £1 million at the time of authorisation; and all UK-incorporated institutions must include such numbers of non-executive directors as the Bank deems appropriate.

Fortunately, for would-be applicants and outside commentators alike, a detailed explanation of how the Bank interprets these criteria is provided in a 'statement of principles' published by the Bank in May 1988 and readers are recommended to consult this document.

The assessment of capital adequacy

An institution has to meet certain prudential standards, as prescribed by the Bank, the first and perhaps most significant being those relating to capital adequacy. The Bank's general approach to the assessment of the capital adequacy of banks was first outlined in a paper issued in September 1980 entitled 'The measurement of capital'. This has since been amended in June 1986 and the definition of capital updated by the Bank in March 1986 in *Subordinated loan capital issued by recognised by banks and licensed deposit-takers*. Further amendments to supervisory practice will be necessitated by the implementation of the Bank for International Settlements (BIS) capital adequacy 'rules' agreed in July 1988.

The definition of capital

As at early 1989, the Bank defines capital for capital adequacy assessment purposes as net assets – paid-up capital and reserves for a body corporate – plus 'allowable' subordinated loan stocks, as defined in March 1986. Acceptable subordinated loan stock comes in two forms: term subordinated debt and perpetual debt. To rank as *primary capital* the definition of capital favoured by UK and US regulators is supposed to comprise only the highest quality components, so subordinated loan stock has to be in the form of perpetual debt which satisfies fairly exacting conditions. There is a limit on the amount of 'qualifying' perpetual debt which may be counted as primary capital.

Although term subordinated debt does not rank as primary capital it is included, subject to limits and restrictions, in what the Bank calls the *capital base*. This definition of capital plays an important part in the Bank's quantitative assessment of capital adequacy. However, the Bank has switched attention to the new definition which comprises the sum of Tier 1 ('core') and Tier 2 ('supplementary') capital. The former group of capital elements comprises ordinary paid-up share capital, disclosed reserves and non-cumulative, perpetual preferred stock, and is included in the capital base without limit. The latter group comprises undisclosed reserves, asset revaluation reserves, general provisions, hybrid capital instruments and subordinated term debt, and can only constitute, in aggregate, a maximum of

100 percent of Tier 1 capital (i.e. 50 percent of the capital base). And, the inclusion of 'qualifying' subordinated term debt is subject to a maximum of 50 percent of Tier 1 capital (i.e. 25 percent of the capital base) and limits are also placed on the inclusion of general provisions within the capital base.

In accordance with the discretion allowed it under the rules, the Bank has indicated that the 'qualifying criteria' applying to subordinated loan stock will remain, that asset revaluation reserves in the form of latent gains on unrealised securities will be disallowed, and that general provisions which reflect lower valuations of assets, notably against Less Developed Country (LDC) debt, will not count at all as Tier 2 capital. In the meantime, the Bank will allow qualifying general provisions to be included in Tier 2 capital up to a level of 1.5 percent of weighted risk assets up to the end of 1992 and 1.25 percent thereafter.

The Bank's capital requirements

In assessing capital adequacy, the Bank seeks to take account of *all* possible risks of loss to which an institution may be exposed. Each is analysed on the basis of standardised returns submitted on a regular basis to the Bank, and some are subject to formal assessment: *credit risk* according to a model outlined in the Bank's paper of September 1980 (amended March and June 1986); and foreign exchange risk according to the Bank's papers on *Foreign currency exposure* (April 1981) and *Foreign currency options* (April 1984). The risk analysis is undertaken on both a consolidated and unconsolidated basis, the former to capture exposures arising in connected companies and the latter to allow for an assessment of the appropriateness of the distribution of capital within the group. Finally, special reporting requirements for large exposures are used to monitor concentration risk.

The Bank's purpose is to provide a subjective evaluation of capital adequacy which takes full account of all risks the institution is exposed to and the ability of its management to handle those risks. The results of its deliberations are encapsulated in the form of a minimum capital ratio – the so-called trigger *risk asset ratio* (RAR) – which is prescribed, on a case-by-case basis, for each authorised institution. The RAR is derived by expressing an institution's *adjusted capital base* as a percentage of its *adjusted total of risk assets* (ATRA). The denominator, in turn, is derived by summing the products of the nominal values of each balance sheet item and their corresponding *risk weights*, according to a classification system established by the Bank. The Bank expects each institution to maintain its RAR at a margin above the trigger level. This higher ratio is known as the 'target' RAR.

Under the BIS 'rules' the RAR methodology will continue to be applied, although a new set of risk weights will apply and an attempt will be made to incorporate all off-balance sheet (OBS) activities within the RAR calculation. This will be done by converting the notional principal amounts of OBS activities (excluding interest rate and foreign exchange rate related instruments) into on-balance sheet loan equivalents (the so-called *deemed credit risk equivalents*) by multiplying by the 'appropriate' *conversion factors*. These loan equivalents will then be slotted into the basic weighting framework according to the nature of the counterparty ('obligor') involved but, occasionally, according to the remaining maturity of the obligation or to the nature of the qualifying collateral or guarantees. Special treatment, however, is afforded interest rate and foreign exchange rate related instruments, such as single currency swaps, forward rate agreements, cross-currency swaps, forward foreign currency contracts and interest rate and foreign currency options purchased by a bank.

As before, a two-stage process is used to transform the notional principal amounts into risk-weighted amounts. The notional principal amounts will first be converted into on-balance sheet loan equivalents and then assigned a risk weight. The first stage of the process, however, differs from that described above.

For interest rate and foreign exchange rate related instruments, the 'loan equivalents' will be measured as the sum of two components:

1. The current exposure faced by the institution, which equals the 'mark-to-market' value of the contract,
2. An estimate of the potential future credit exposure faced over the life of the instrument owing to fluctuations in interest rates or exchange rates.

The second component will be calculated by multiplying the notional principal amounts by the 'appropriate' conversion factors.

In this manner, the Bank attempts to 'capture' all on- and off-balance sheet activities within the RAR calculation and, consistent with the BIS 'rules', ensure that all prescribed 'trigger' ratios are at or above the minimum of 8 percent accepted by the signatories to the Basle Committee's document. This will provide a degree of reassurance that an institution is financially sound in the sense that capital holdings will, to a degree, be related to perceived (credit) risk thereby, hopefully, allowing the institution to absorb any losses which unfortunately may materialise without precipitating a winding-up.

The assessment of liquidity adequacy

The bank's chief concern in assessing liquidity adequacy is to seek to ensure that banks are able to meet their contractual obligations, on both sides of the balance sheet, as they fall due. To this end, the Bank attempts to ensure that management adopts a 'prudent' mix of liquidity forms – e.g. cash, readily-liquefiable assets, asset maturity monies, a diversified deposit base and other borrowing sources – appropriate to the business undertaken, that 'appropriate' maturity-matching policies are adopted, and that satisfactory monitoring and control systems are in place to allow for continuous assessment by the management of the bank's liquidity position.

The success of the process lies heavily on the assessment of management quality, as with the assessment of capital adequacy. Individual business characteristics, including any potential liquidity problems which could arise in group or other connected companies, are fully taken into account in the overall subjective evaluation.

The treatment of foreign currency operations

In assessing foreign exchange position risk the Bank is concerned with all exposures arising from any uncovered foreign currency position, including those incurred through the writing of options business, in any currency. Net positions in single currencies, including sterling, are considered alongside the aggregate net position in all currencies.

The Bank agrees dealing position 'guidelines' with each bank, on an individual basis, and seeks to ensure that banks' internal controls are adequate to allow for effective and continuous monitoring of exposures against the agreed guidelines. The guidelines agreed with an individual institution will reflect that institution's expertise in foreign exchange operations and its particular business mix and circumstances.

The Bank has stated (April 1981) that, generally speaking, UK-incorporated banks experienced in foreign exchange operations can expect to agree the following guidelines:

1. A limit on the net open dealing position in any one currency of 10 percent of the adjusted capital base (as defined for capital adequacy assessment purposes).
2. A limit on the net short open dealing (spot and forward) positions of all currencies taken together of 15 percent of the adjusted capital base.

The treatment of large exposures

Under the Banking Act 1987 all UK-incorporated banks and UK banking groups are required to notify the Bank of any 'exposure' to a single non-bank party or group of closely-related non-bank parties which is in excess of 10 percent of the adjusted capital base (as defined for the assessment of capital adequacy). Prior notification is required of transactions which would raise exposure above the 25 percent threshold. The definition of 'exposure' used for this purpose is the sum of all claims plus undrawn facilities, contingent liabilities, other counterparty risks and equity holdings (for full details, see Bank of England, September 1987).

The Bank's policy, as set out in *Large Exposures Undertaken by Institutions Authorised Under the Banking Act* 1987 (Bank of England, September 1987), is that such exposures should not normally exceed 10 percent of the adjusted capital base and those that do will be thoroughly investigated. Except in the most exceptional circumstances, the Bank will not sanction exposures in excess of the 25 percent threshold. Exceptions to this rule, however, do apply, embracing the following:

(a) exposures to other banks with a maturity of up to one year;
(b) exposures to overseas central governments;
(c) exposures of up to one year to group financial companies;
(d) exposures secured by cash or an ECGD guarantee or British government stocks;
(e) underwriting exposures incurred by 'experts' (see *Large Underwriting Exposures* (Bank of England, February 1988) for full details);
(f) in the case of bank subsidiaries, exposures guaranteed by the parent bank.

For those banks which are allowed to run a number of exposures in excess of the 10 percent threshold or any in excess of the 25 percent threshold or which have particular concentrations of risk, the Bank will normally require additional capital to be held, the amount being dependent on a number of factors:

1. On the standing of the borrower.
2. The nature of the bank's relationship with the borrower.
3. The nature and extent of security taken against the exposure.
4. The bank's expertise in the particular area of activity.
5. The number of such exposures, their individual size and nature.

The assessment of the adequacy of provisions

Requirements for 'adequate' provisions derive from both the 'prudent conduct' authorisation criterion established in the Banking Act 1987 and from the Companies Act 1985. To fulfill these obligations, authorised institutions have to make provisions for *inter alia* bad and doubtful debts, expected losses on contingents and tax liabilities, losses and liabilities to be recognised in accordance with accepted accounting standards (as set out in the *Statements of Standard Accounting Practice* published by the Institute of Chartered Accountants, various dates).

The assessment of country risk

While accepting that it is the primary responsibility of management to measure, assess and control country risks, the Bank, nevertheless, seeks to ensure that each authorised institution adopts suitable risk assessment systems, that adequate resources are devoted to the task of assessing risk and that adequate internal controls exist for controlling and monitoring exposures. The provision of statistical returns on such exposures and regular discussions with management assist the Bank in this policy.

In assessing exposures, the Bank will pay particular regard to their size and nature in relation to the institution's capital and provisions; the larger the exposure to problem debtors and the smaller the level of provisions, the higher the likely risk:asset ratio requirement.

Ownership rules

The 'O'Brien rules' restricted shareholding links between recognised brokers in foreign exchange and currency deposits and banks or other principals in the market to less than 10 percent. They were removed in November 1986, but certain restraints on ownership remain.

Informal restraints relate to the guidelines, practices and 'understandings' which exist between the Bank and the relevant government departments governing the permissible degree of interlocking ownership with non-bank financial institutions. These are designed to limit the risks associated with connected lending and cross-contamination. The formal 'rules' relate to the powers vested in HM Treasury, the Office of Fair Trading, the Monopolies and Mergers Commission and the Bank.

Under the Banking Act 1987 the Bank possesses powers, and considerable discretion within those powers, to exercise influence over the ownership and control of UK-authorised institutions. A prospective 'shareholder controller' – i.e. someone who owns or exercises control over the voting rights associated with over 15 percent of the institution's equity – has to meet the Bank's 'fit and proper' criterion. Once over this hurdle, a prospective shareholder controller may then fall foul of the reciprocity clause inserted into the Banking Act to allow the Bank, on the direction of the Treasury, to block moves made by those institutions incorporated in a country which does not give reciprocal rights to UK residents and firms. And finally, even if both of these obstacles can be overcome, a foreign stake-builder may have its ambitions dashed by the Monopolies and Mergers Commission, on the advice of the Office of Fair Trading, on 'national interest' considerations if the predatory ambitions extend to gaining full control. This fate befell the Hong Kong and Shanghai Banking Corporation in its attempted merger with the Royal Bank of Scotland in 1982.

Despite this array of impediments which can be placed in the way of prospective foreign predators the authorities are not averse, on principle, to foreign participation in UK banks. The Bank is, however, determined to ensure that the 'core' of the financial system (i.e. the payments mechanism and the supply of credit) remains in the hands of domestic institutions and that a strong British presence in the UK banking system is maintained. Accordingly, prospective foreign bank predators are likely to be 'warned off' if their aspirations relate to securing control of the major UK banks, and prospective non-bank predators are unlikely to even come under 'starters orders', such is the Bank's concern to limit the risks associated with cross-contamination.

Deposit insurance arrangements

All authorised institutions are obliged to contribute to a fund managed by the Deposit Protection Board to provide for the compensation of depositors who suffer losses as a result of a collapse of a UK-authorised institution. The contributions are subject to a statutory ceiling of 0.3 percent of an institution's sterling deposit base' and are size-related. The current minimum and maximum amounts applying are £10,000 and £300,000, respectively, although special arrangements allow for the imposition of supplementary levies – up to the statutory ceiling – should the need arise.

Under the Deposit Protection Scheme, all corporate and personal sector depositors (bar those associated with the institution) are 'insured' to the tune of 75 percent of the first £20,000 of their sterling deposits held with each and every authorised institution.

The Bank of England's regulation of banks' securities operations

The operations of bank subsidiaries engaged in specialist operations in the gilt-edged market – market-making, interdealer broking or money-broking – are subject to special supervisory arrangements. For each of the above participants in the gilt-edged market the Bank seeks to ensure that exposures are not disproportionate to their capital bases, and that internal control and monitoring arrangements are adequate to allow the institutions to ensure that this situation is maintained on a continuous basis. To this end, the capital base will be carefully defined for an institution, 'guidelines' for measuring (credit and/or position) risk exposure will be established and rigorous reporting requirements will be imposed. Moreover, the Bank insists that such subsidiaries operate at arm's length from their parents and related entities and with their own dedicated capital, which cannot readily be withdrawn at the discretion of the parent.

Further responsibilities for the regulation of banks' securities operations fall on the Bank by virtue of the 'lead regulator' role assumed under the Financial Services Act 1986 for the regulation of 'investment business'. According to the *Memoranda of Understanding* (MoU) signed, in March 1988, by the Bank on the one hand and the Securities and Investments Board (SIB), The Securities Association (TSA) and the Investment Managers' Regulatory Organisation (IMRO) on the other, the Bank, at least for the time being, acts as 'lead regulator' while the financial services supervisor [i.e. the self-regulatory organisation (SRO)] is required to monitor compliance by the institutions with its 'conduct of business' rules.

As lead regulator, the Bank is usually responsible for monitoring the capital adequacy of an authorised institution on behalf of the SIB/SRO. For banks heavily involved in securities trading, the arrangements governing the split of supervisory responsibilities can be quite complex. For example, in respect of those banks which are members of TSA, the Bank informs TSA whenever a bank's capital falls below a certain level determined by taking account of both the risk:asset ratio imposed by the Bank on its banking business and the TSA's position and counterparty risk requirements for securities trading. The Bank also assesses the capital adequacy of each such bank in the traditional way, using its standard definition of capital.

In some instances, however, the SIB/SRO may be responsible for monitoring capital adequacy. This is the case, for example, where a bank's business is almost exclusively securities trading or investment-related, or where non- 'investment business' is negligible. In such instances, the SIB/ SRO will calculate the bank's capital ratio on behalf of the Bank, using the Bank's standard definition of capital and in accordance with rules agreed between itself and the Bank.

The regulation of banks' activities in the 'wholesale' markets

A Wholesale Markets Supervision Division (WMSD) was set up within the Bank in 1986 following the government's decision to make the Bank, rather than the SIB or an SRO, responsible for the supervision of certain wholesale markets in the bullion, foreign exchange and sterling money-markets. Supervision is exercised, on a non-statutory basis, by this department over the market-makers and brokers which act in these markets according to the Bank's April 1988 'Grey Paper', as amended by subsequent market notices.

In brief, supervision involves 'listed' institutions (i.e. those eligible to engage in transactions in these wholesale markets) in meeting the Bank's capital adequacy requirements and abiding by both the letter and the spirit of the 'London Code of Conduct', a document drawn up by the Bank, with the aid of practitioners, to establish general principles of good market conduct and conventions relating to market terminology and definitions and certain aspects of trading. The approach taken to capital adequacy assessment is in line, where relevant, with agreements ('Memoranda of Understanding') reached with the SIB/SROs on the division of supervisory responsibilities.

The supervision of banking groups

The Bank's supervision of banking groups is based mainly on the consolidated statistical returns and the annual reports and accounts of group companies. In addition, however, in order to ensure that supervision is 'cost effective', the Bank has adopted the 'lead regulator' principle wherever necessary.

The Bank's policy on consolidated supervision is designed to provide an assessment of the overall strength of a banking group and of the potential impact on a bank of the group's non-banking operations. Usually, the Bank will require submission of consolidated financial statements, with different parts of the group being included in the consolidated returns according to

Bank instructions. The Bank's decision as to which parts of the group should
be included in the statistical reporting will rest, in turn, on a study of the nature
of the particular activities engaged in, the position occupied by each company
within the overall group structure and the supervision exercised by other UK
supervisory bodies. Where the Bank does not require consolidation of returns
of group companies it may, nevertheless, still request information about group
company activities if the risks of contaminating the bank(s) within the group
are viewed with concern.

Concluding comments

The material presented above explains the current approach taken by the
Bank to the prudential regulation and supervision of institutions 'authorised'
under The Banking Act 1987, but this will remain subject to change in the
light of developments in both domestic and international financial markets.
Moreover, commitments assumed by virtue of membership of international
policymaking organisations (e.g. the Basle Committee of Supervisors and the
European Community) will increasingly shape domestic policy as the
pressures for convergence in supervisory practice intensify.

As for the Bank's ability to retain its traditional reliance upon its moral
authority in discharging its supervisory obligations, the evidence would
suggest that it will face an uphill battle. The legal challenges mounted against
many of the remaining forms of non-statutory controls evident in the UK
financial system – such as the Takeover Panel in its administration of the
Takeover Code – show no sign of waning and the deterrent effect of 'official'
reprimands meted out by these non-statutory bodies is at best questionable.
The judicial review successfully sought by Lonhro of the Department of
Trade and Industry's decision in 1985 not to refer the takeover of the House
of Fraser by the Al Fayed brothers to the Monopolies and Mergers
Commission provides yet further evidence of the ever-increasing litigiousness
of the market-place, raising the spectre of the Bank's administration of the
voluntary 'London Code of Conduct' one day being tested in the courts.
Moreover, recent events at Equiticorp, the New Zealand company which
acquired a 61 percent stake in the UK merchant bank Guinness Mahon as a
result of the purchase of a similar-sized stake in the Guinness Peat Group in
September 1987 and which called in the receivers in January 1989, have
resurrected anxiety in some quarters about the Bank's judgement.

While the Bank can legitimately claim that the old legislation (The Banking
Act 1979 was in force at the time) did not allow it to block Equiticorp's move to
secure a controlling stake (its stake in April 1987 was only 24 percent) in
Guinness Mahon, this did not preclude the exercise of moral suasion which,
apparently, was used to deter Robert Maxwell, the publisher, from pursuing a
rival bid for the Guinness Peat Group. A vote of confidence in Equiticorp
from the Reserve Bank of New Zealand no doubt provided reassurance to the

Bank at the time about the integrity of the controllers but, by August 1988, circumstances had changed to such an extent that the Bank was moved to ask Equiticorp, in secret, to sell its stake in Guinness Mahon. The Bank also sought to ensure the independent management of the bank in the interim and that exposures to the rest of the group would not be entertained by the bank.

It would appear that, for whatever reason, 'undesirables' were able to secure control of a British merchant bank, and some of the political 'flak' will undoubtedly rub off on the Bank. Coming in the wake of the Johnson Matthey Bankers fiasco of 1984 this is unfortunate, for it may yet further weaken the esteem with which the Bank is held in some quarters, thereby exacerbating the acute pressures already faced by the Bank in its struggle to retain moral authority as an independent source of supervisory power.

17

❧

THE PANEL ON
TAKEOVERS AND MERGERS

ANTONY BEEVOR

The Takeover Panel is not concerned with competition policy or other aspects of the public interest such as regional, social or employment policies. Nor is it concerned with the financial merits of a particular offer – that is for the shareholders to decide. The Panel regulates the conduct of an offer. Its job is to ensure fair treatment for shareholders and a level playing-field between the protagonists. The Panel seeks to achieve these objectives through the City Code on Takeovers and Mergers. The Code was first written 20 years ago and now comprises 10 General Principles and 38 Rules. However, it can be summed in four broad objectives which constitute the original underlying philosophy of the Panel and the Code.

The first has already been mentioned. The Code seeks to ensure equality of treatment between shareholders large and small. The second is to ensure adequate and timely information to enable shareholders to decide on the merits of an offer. The third is to ensure a fair market in the shares of companies which are involved in takeovers. It is sometimes suggested that market dealings in companies that are subject to takeovers should be suspended and thus the risk of market manipulation would be eliminated. That might be an easy way out, but it is desirable that an active market should be setting a value both on shares the bidder may be offering and on the target company's own shares, thus acting as a barometer against which the latter company's shareholders can assess the offer. The fourth objective of the Code is to ensure that neither target companies nor their directors take action which would frustrate an offer against the wishes of their shareholders.

The essential spirit of the Code is set out in these four objectives. They underlie the 10 General Principles which form the opening section of the Code. The 38 Rules of the Code which form the bulk of the book are in the nature of examples of these principles in practice.

Perhaps the best-known rule of the Code is Rule 9, which requires a person who acquires 30 percent or more of the voting rights in a company to make a cash offer to all other shareholders at the highest price paid by it in the previous 12 months. That is the classic example of the equal treatment of all shareholders. Control of a company cannot be bought by paying a super price to the controlling shareholder and leaving the remainder in an effective minority to the new controller; for this purpose 30 percent of the voting rights is regarded as conferring effective control. Rule 9 is important, in that it stops the need for a number of the more vigorous minority protection devices that are seen in other jurisdictions. It has been argued that it is because the US system lacks the equivalent of a 30 percent rule that poison pills are needed to help the boards of defending companies negotiate a fair deal for all shareholders.

A second important rule is Rule 11, which requires that when shares carrying 15 percent or more of the voting rights of a particular class of shares in a company have been acquired for cash by an offeror during or within 12 months prior to the commencement of an offer period, then the offer must include a cash alternative for all the shares of that class at the highest price paid by the offeror during that period. The Rule is another example of the fair treatment principle at work. A special deal in terms of cash cannot be offered to important shareholders when perhaps slightly suspect paper is all that is being offered to the others. Thirdly, and in similar vein, Rule 6 states that if an offeror purchases shares in the offeree company at a price higher than the then value of its offer, the offer must be increased accordingly. Under Rule 16 favourable deals for particular shareholders are prohibited. Again, the equal treatment principle at work.

Another important rule, Rule 3, is derived from the information principle. The offeree company must appoint a competent independent adviser whose views on the offer must be made known to all shareholders so that they have the views not just of the board, some of whom may possibly have vested interests in the outcome, but also the views of an independent expert. In most cases, but by no means all, that means a merchant bank.

Rule 19 states *inter alia* that the same information must be given to competing offerors by an offeree company. This is an application of the anti-frustration principle. An offeree company is not allowed to give the favoured suitor an unfair advantage by providing it with information designed to enable it to pay a high and generous price, whilst at the same time a less favoured rival is deprived of that information, making it more difficult for the latter to compete.

Finally there is the extremely important and valuable Rule 8 which, together with other disclosure rules, requires prompt disclosure of market dealings by all relevant parties. This, of course, is the principal way in which the Panel seeks to ensure a fair market in shares of companies subject to bids. These requirements, which create significant administrative burdens for stockbrokers and others who deal regularly in shares of companies in bids, have become more onerous in the last two years, and at the same time the Panel's system for monitoring them has become more efficient, in a way which is described briefly below.

The development of the Code over the years is interesting. The four fundamental principles have been the basis of the Code since it started more than 20 years ago. The number of rules has increased little. There were 35 rules in the first version of the Code. There are now 38. However, the rule-book is thicker because many individual rules have appended to them notes setting out interpretation and practices which have become established by cases which have been brought before the Panel or the Panel executive. 'Case law' has developed the Code. As well as the Code itself, the Panel administers the Rules Governing Substantial Acquisitions of Shares. These were introduced by the Council for the Securities Industry but have always been administered by the Panel. They are designed to slow the rate at which substantial holdings may be built in companies. They do not apply to a purchaser who has announced a general offer for the company whose shares are being brought.

A crucial characteristic of the Code is flexibility. The Code is not statute or created under authority delegated by Parliament. Its non-statutory nature permits a flexibility of interpretation and a speed of amendment which, in the view of the Panel and many others, is essential in the fast moving field of takeovers. Central to the system is the concept that it is the spirit of the Code which must be observed, and not just the letter. How this operates in practice is fundamental to understanding how the Panel works.

In December 1987 British Petroleum (BP) announced a bid for Britoil. Britoil had a 'golden share' owned by the British Government, which provided that however many votes all the ordinary share capital exercised on a particular occasion, the golden share was entitled to exercise one more. Rule 10 of the Code, which provides, in broad terms, that a bidder cannot declare an offer unconditional unless it achieves 50 percent of the outstanding voting rights, was not written with such golden shares in mind. The Panel had to decide how to interpret that Rule in the light of the particular circumstances of Britoil. The view was taken that Rule 10 would be satisfied if 50 percent of the ordinary share capital (excluding the golden share) was acquired. BP was prepared to proceed on that basis and the Britoil shareholders were thereby enabled to have the opportunity to consider an offer which, in the event, they found attractive.

In August 1988 the Panel was asked to waive the strict requirement of Rule 35 (that neither a bidder whose offer has lapsed nor any person who is or was acting in concert with it should make a new offer for the same target within 12 months) to permit Grand Metropolitan to bid on its own for Irish Distillers after the European Commission had indicated it was likely to block the earlier bid by a consortium of which Grand Metropolitan had been a member. The Panel felt that shareholders had not in the event had a proper opportunity to consider the earlier offer and that therefore the protection for target companies against being continually under siege should in these unprecedented circumstances be varied, provided Grand Metropolitan's new offer was restricted to a very tight timetable which, in the absence of a rival bid, had the effect of extending the original 'siege' period by only 17 days.

These cases demonstrate, first, that the takeover world regularly produces situations which could not reasonably be envisaged by the authors of any rule-book, and secondly that the Panel feels able to respond to such situations by modifying the strict letter of its rules to achieve the result that it believes most fairly reflects the underlying Principles of the Code in the particular circumstances.

In addition to this flexibility of interpretation, the non-statutory regime also allows more rapid amendment to the Code than if it were a statute or even a statutory instrument. A recent example was the important and radical introduction of the concept of exempt market-makers which followed the formation of financial conglomerates and was designed to cater for the Code consequences of merchant banks owning market-makers. If, because they belonged to the same group, such market-makers were held to be acting in concert with an offeror client of the corporate finance department, serious consequences would follow. If in their market-making operations the bank bought shares which took the aggregate of the bank's and bidder's holdings over 15 percent, the bidder could find itself with an obligation to make a cash offer or perhaps even to increase its offer. Such a result would have risked disrupting the market and would have had severe consequences on the market-making business. The Panel therefore developed the concept of the exempt market-maker which is now part of the Code. If exemption is granted the actions of the market-maker do not have Code consequences (other than disclosure) for the bidding client of the related corporate finance department.

Another important recent amendment is the 1 percent Disclosure Rule. It became apparent during 1986 that a greater degree of transparency in the market in shares involved in takeovers was necessary. The Panel therefore introduced a rule requiring disclosure of dealings by any holder of 1 percent or more of a class of share of a company that is involved in a takeover bid. A large number of institutions customarily have more than 1 percent of the companies they invest in and therefore the volume of disclosures has increased markedly.

So it is a regular occurrence for the Panel to be confronted by situations not specifically envisaged by the authors of the Code and to have to decide what to do about it. It is the flexible nature of the system which allows the Panel to deal with such situations fairly and efficiently. In the world of takeovers, populated by clever and inventive people, ready to find a way round Rules, it is important for the Panel to have flexibility and to be able to go back to the spirit, and in particular to the four basic Principles, in deciding how the Code should be interpreted. However, there is a price to be paid for this accent on flexibility. This is the need that the Panel executive recognises for a high quality advisory service, so that the parties who are affected by the Code and those who are advising them may know how the Code is to be applied in cases that are not expressly dealt with in the rule-book.

The Panel executive has a staff of approximately twenty-five centred on nine assistant secretaries who deal with daily telephone enquiries. With one exception these assistant secretaries are professionals in their late twenties or early thirties on two years' secondment from a variety of employers, notably accountants, clearing banks and stockbrokers, but also the Department of Trade and Industry and the Bank of England. The assistant secretaries have the main burden of communicating with practitioners and parties to bids, usually by telephone. They receive initial enquiries and they disseminate answers. Above them is a senior level of six executives. Three bear the title of secretaries to the Panel and two of those secretaries are lawyers, probably at junior partner level, on secondment from firms of City solicitors. There are two Deputy Directors-General, both of whom are permanent, and the Director-General, who has with only one exception been a merchant banker, again on two years' secondment. This blend of secondees and permanent staff is very important. The system enables the Panel to maintain a very high calibre of personnel, since employers have been ready to release some of their most talented staff, to the benefit, it is hoped, both of the individual and the employer. The workload of the panel can be heavy and a regular turnover of executives helps to maintain a freshness of approach and enthusiasm for the role which makes such pressures tolerable. At the same time, the permanent members provide continuity on which the temporary members depend heavily.

The day-to-day procedures of the Panel executive and the Panel are designed to combine speed with consistency and fairness. An assistant secretary may be able to give an immediate answer to the question he is asked, but if it is in any way non-routine it will be debated internally – perhaps at the Panel executive's regular ten o'clock morning meeting. If possible, the views of any opposing party will be invited. A party who is dissatisfied with a ruling of the executive can appeal that ruling to the full Panel, and it is also to the full Panel that the executive refers breaches of the Code for disciplinary action. The procedures of the full Panel are set out in the introduction to the Code and have been drawn up carefully in order that proceedings comply with the principles of natural justice. The full Panel comprises a cross-section of senior City and business figures. A party before the Panel has its case heard by its peers and most shades of opinion are represented. Thus to describe the Panel as a self-regulatory organisation does not do it justice. The Panel is not just composed of merchant bankers: it contains a very broad church of financial and business opinion as well as a few members appointed by the Governor of the Bank of England, including the Chairman and the two Deputy Chairmen, who do not represent any particular interest. This breadth of representation is an important source of the Panel's authority.

In disciplinary cases and other cases of hardship a right of appeal from the Panel is available to the Panel's Appeal Committee whose Chairman is a retired Law Lord.

Rightly, and as with other public administrative bodies, the proceedings of the Panel are open to judicial review by the Courts. This has occurred twice.

The first of these, the Datafin case, involved rival bids for McCorquodale in December 1986. The Master of the Rolls, then Sir John Donaldson, commented favourably in that case on the Panel's procedures and on the importance of the service which it provides in the context of takeovers. He suggested that the Court would be slow to reverse a decision of the Panel, particularly when that decision had already been acted on in the market-place. The Guinness case was also the subject of a Court of Appeal judgement in July 1988. The Court seemed inclined to look for a still higher standard of procedure when the urgency of a contemporary takeover was absent, but unanimously affirmed that the Panel had caused no injustice to Guinness. Judgments like these demonstrate the Court's recognition of the system. They provide the Panel with useful guidance on its procedures and at the same time lend significant authority to the Panel and to its judgments.

It is important to appreciate that, despite its non-statutory constitution, the Panel has a measure of statutory recognition which is gaining increasing importance in the context of enforcing the Panel's rules and decisions. The Panel itself was the subject of a fundamental review by the Department of Trade and Industry (DTI) and others in the Spring of 1987 to decide whether, in the light of the then changes that were being made to the regulation of financial services by the Financial Services Act, any changes in the constitution of the Panel were appropriate.

The recommendation from that review, which was accepted at the highest level in Government, was that the Panel's constitution should remain undisturbed. Following that review, the Panel's powers have been strengthened. The Panel is designated under the relevant legislation to receive from the DTI information which the DTI obtains under Section 447 of the 1985 Companies Act, and also information from regulatory bodies under the Financial Services Act. Secondly, the rules of the Securities and Investments Board, and of the relevant SROs, provide that firms authorised to carry on investment business should not act for clients which are not prepared to comply with the Code. Similarly, the same rules provide that breaches of the Code by practitioners may be taken into account by an SRO in considering whether a particular institution is fit and proper to be authorised to carry on investment business. Lastly, the rules of The Securities Association, the SRO to which stockbrokers and corporate finance departments of merchant banks belong, require members to supply the Panel with information about market dealings and other matters relevant to the Panel's work.

The Panel has always had the support of the various organisations which make up the financial community and it has thus always been able, as the introduction of the Code puts it, effectively to deny the facilities of the securities market to those who were not prepared to comply. As a result, the Panel has in practice experienced very little difficulty in enforcing its rules in the 5,000 or so cases that it has dealt with over more than 20 years, but the arrangements described are none the less welcome reinforcement.

Another recent development, an important one because of the perceived abuses which have occurred through various transactions in bid stocks in the stock-market, is the Panel's ability to monitor market dealings on a daily basis through the computerised records of The Stock Exchange. This has proved important in enforcing compliance with the expanded disclosure requirements of Rule 8 of the Code, in watching for abuses of the 'exempt' status of the market-making and funds management divisions of financial institutions and generally in checking for breaches of the Code by parties to a takeover through the stock-market. The Panel executive now contains a specialist team, headed by a secondee from the Surveillance Division of The Stock Exchange, whose full-time role is to monitor such dealings. It has become a regular event for brokers to receive enquiries as to why transactions have not been disclosed and, occasionally, for a more detailed account of the reasons for a particular transaction. The same team is also vigilant in seeking out relevant information and if appropriate requiring an announcement under Rule 2 of the Code where there is evidence of speculation in the market but where no announcement has been made.

The field of takeovers is not an easy one to regulate, and it is likely to get more difficult as the securities industry becomes more and more global. No regulatory authority in any field can guarantee 100 percent compliance, but the Panel's flexibility, derived from the non-statutory nature of its system combined with the statutory recognition described above, lends support to its claim to be the best of the systems that are operating around the world in this difficult area. Most of those who operate in the field in London seem to share that view.

PART FIVE

❧

THE GLOBAL DIMENSION

18

❦

JAPAN

THE VISCOUNT TRENCHARD

Just as it is becoming more difficult to define precisely the term 'merchant banking' even in the United Kingdom and present or former Commonwealth countries, which are the only group of countries which commonly use the term, it is even more difficult in Japan. The financial and corporate system there before World War II had certain limited similarities to that of West Germany and it has been heavily influenced by the United States during the post-war period.

Although in practice the distinction between different types of Japanese institutions has become blurred in certain areas, and the law is slowly changing to grant recognition to the reality, the functions of the different types of institutions remain clearly defined. Each type may operate only on receipt of a licence or licences permitting the operation of certain distinct lines of financial business and the provision of certain distinct financial services. Parts of what we call 'merchant banking' in the United Kingdom are undertaken by securities companies, parts by 'city' banks and long-term banks (commercial banks) and parts by trust banks.

Article 65 of the Commercial Code of Japan, modelled on the US Glass-Steagall Act, requires the separation of banking business from securities business. This Article lies at the heart of the Japanese financial system. The Ministry of Finance includes entirely distinct Banking and Securities Bureaux, which separately regulate banks and securities companies.

There are three distinct types of commercial bank in Japan. City banks have traditionally been the major source of funds for Japanese industry. There are 13 city banks, some of which are direct descendents of the old Zaibatsu banks such as Mitsubishi, Mitsui and Sumitomo. There are 64 regional banks, which are smaller than the enormous city banks and which play almost no role in international business. There were in 1988, 81 foreign commercial banks in Japan operating a total of 115 branches. In terms of assets, they represent roughly 3 percent of the Japanese banking industry.

Other types of bank include the three long-term credit banks, the Industrial Bank of Japan, the Long-term Credit Bank of Japan and Nippon Credit Bank. The traditional main activity of these banks was to provide long-term funds to major companies. Now many of the largest companies, such as Matsushita and Toyota are themselves jokingly referred to as banks in view of their surplus liquidity and the differentiation of function between these three banks and the city banks is gradually disappearing.

Besides the commercial banks there are seven Japanese and, since 1985, nine licensed foreign trust banks authorised to conduct trust business in Japan. There are also over 60 sogo banks which are mutual loans and savings banks, some of which are now converting themselves into commercial banks, and three specialised co-operative banks.

There are some 240 Japanese securities companies, of which by far the largest and most powerful are the 'big four' securities companies: Nomura, Daiwa, Nikko and Yamaichi. There are 45 foreign securities companies operating through licensed branches in Japan (see Table 18.1). There are 22 foreign members among the 115 members of Tokyo Stock Exchange (TSE). No foreign members were admitted before 1986 when six joined, the remaining sixteen being invited to take their seats in 1988, at a cost of around Y1,200 million each. Securities companies in Japan underwrite and distribute new issues of equities and bonds and trade in them for their own account and for the account of their customers. The large securities companies have, among their subsidiaries, investment trust companies.

Before the Investment Advisory Law of 1986 there were no regulations governing investment advisory business. Many banks, securities companies and other Japanese and foreign institutions have opened investment management or investment advisory companies under the new law.

Many UK merchant banks had old relationships with Japan. They had underwritten sterling bond issues for the Japanese Government in London before the First World War. Much of the finance for the construction of the Tokyo – Yokohama railway had been raised in London. Since the 1960s some merchant banks have been active lenders to Japanese trading companies outside Japan. In addition, they were involved, together with the UK clearing banks, in the 'impact loan' business. Impact loans were foreign currency loans to Japanese resident corporations, and used to be a lucrative business for foreign financial institutions. This business has almost entirely disappeared for two main reasons. First, Japanese banks, which had been restricted from involvement in this business, were permitted to engage in it by the revised foreign exchange law of 1980. And secondly, Japanese corporations increasingly turned to foreign currency denominated bonds in the international capital markets as a cheaper substitute for impact loans.

Kleinwort Benson was the first British merchant bank to establish a representative office in Tokyo, which it did in 1970. Within a few years, S.G. Warburg, Schroder Wagg, Baring Brothers and Morgan Grenfell followed suit and many others, including the merchant banking subsidiaries of the clearing banks, have done so in recent years. The functions of many of the early representative offices were threefold. First, they served as banking

Table 18.1. Foreign securities companies operating in Japan at 31 December 1988
All branches are established in Tokyo unless otherwise indicated.
Each firm is listed in order of its first branch opening in Japan,
thereafter each branch of a given firm is listed in date order.

Date of branch opening	Company	Membership of TSE
July 1972	Merrill Lynch	o
December 1978	Merrill Lynch – Osaka	
November 1985	Merrill Lynch – Nagoya	
March 1988	Merrill Lynch – Yokohama	o
October 1978	Citicorp Vickers	o
January 1980	Prudential Bache	o
June 1980	Smith Barney	o
May 1981	Jardine Fleming	o
September 1982	Salomon Brothers	o
June 1983	Kidder Peabody	o
September 1987	Kidder Peabody – Osaka	o
November 1983	Goldman Sachs	o
June 1984	Morgan Stanley	o
January 1985	S. G. Warburg	o
March 1985	W. I. Carr	o
July 1985	First Boston	
December 1985	Drexel Burnham	
December 1985	Kleinwort Benson	o
March 1986	Schroder	o
April 1986	Hoare Govett	o
April 1986	PaineWebber	o
May 1986	DB Capital Markets (Deutsche Bank)	o
May 1986	Shearson Lehman	o
June 1986	Cazenove	o
September 1986	Baring	o
October 1986	Dresdner ABD Securities (Dresdner Bank)	
October 1986	SBCI (Swiss Bank Corporation)	
October 1986	County Natwest	
December 1986	DG Securities (DG Bank)	
February 1987	SoGen Securities (Société Générale)	
February 1987	UBS Phillips and Drew	
April 1987	Morgan Grenfell	
June 1987	James Capel	
June 1987	Commerz Securities (Commerzbank)	
June 1987	Amro (Amsterdam–Rotterdam Bank)	
June 1987	WESTLB Securities (Westdeutsche Landesbank)	
June 1987	Paribas Capital Markets (Banque Paribas)	
June 1987	Chase Manhattan Securities	
June 1987	Midland Montagu	
September 1987	Barclays de Zoete Wedd	
October 1987	BT Asia (Bankers Trust)	
October 1987	BV Capital Markets (Bayerische Vereinsbank)	
November 1987	JP Morgan (Morgan Guaranty Trust)	
December 1987	Credit Lyonnais Finanz	
December 1987	Manufacturers Hanover Asia	
February 1988	BHF Securities (Berliner Handels und Frankfurter Bank)	
February 1988	Chemical Securities (Chemical Bank)	
April 1988	Smith New Court	
June 1988	BNP Securities (Banque Nationale de Paris)	

liaison offices, to assist their Head Offices in London in negotiations with Japanese banks and corporations offering trade finance and other banking services. Secondly, they assisted their Head Offices in promoting capital market business by offering to lead manage or co-manage Eurobond issues for Japanese companies. Although today it is almost impossible for a non-Japanese institution to obtain a mandate to lead manage a Eurobond issue involving equity, such as the currently popular issues of bonds with equity warrants attached, in the 1970s Japanese securities companies lacked experience and often allowed foreign houses, including British merchant banks, to lead manage their clients' issues. The third main function of the early representative offices was to provide information on the Japanese economy and stock-market to their London investment departments, whose clients were becoming increasingly interested in the Japanese market.

Representative offices in Japan are not actually allowed to conduct business, and no merchant bank established a branch office in Japan until S.G. Warburg upgraded its office in 1984. Kleinwort Benson's and Schroder Wagg's applications to do the same were accepted by the Ministry of Finance the following year. One reason for this hesitation was that the merchant banks were not certain whether they wished to be banks or securities companies in Japan. It became increasingly clear during the early 1980s that securitisation of financial markets was accelerating, and planning for Big Bang in London started. It also became apparent that the British clearing banks and other foreign commercial banks in Japan were generating a pitifully small return on assets employed in Japan. They suffer from the absence of a natural deposit base in Japan and consequently must fund themselves in the interbank market at more expensive rates than their Japanese competitors.

Many commercial banks have recently been allowed to open branches of 50 percent owned securities companies in Japan in addition to their banking branches as a result of the more liberal interpretation of Article 65 by the Ministry of Finance. The outside shareholders in these 50 percent owned ventures are mostly 'sleeping' shareholders who will retain their investments only as long as the law requires them to do so. Pressure from the Japanese banks for relaxation or abolition of Article 65 is increasing.

It became a fairly natural decision for the merchant banks, along with the major international commercial banks and the US investment banks, to establish securities branches in Japan. A list of the 45 foreign securities companies operating branches in Japan, indicating those which have achieved membership of the Tokyo Stock Exchange, is shown in Table 18.1. The operation of a securities branch in Japan is entirely consistent with the strategy adopted by many merchant banks of turning themselves into global investment banks. The Tokyo Stock Exchange is the largest stock exchange in the world, both in terms of turnover and market capitalisation. Osaka Stock Exchange competes with London for third place.

The foreign securities companies in Japan, like Japanese securities companies, are supervised by the securities bureau of the Ministry of Finance and must submit over 40 monthly reports. The majority of them hold all four securities business licences: the licence to underwrite issues of securities; the licence to distribute securities; the licence to deal in securities as principal; and the licence to deal in securities as agent.

The larger foreign securities companies have started a significant business as underwriters of issues of securities in the Japanese domestic market. Kleinwort Benson is one of the first three managing underwriters in the Japanese Government Bond syndicate, and S.G. Warburg is also one of the group of nine foreign securities companies from which three will be selected annually by rotation. Foreign securities companies often participate in issues of convertible bonds in the domestic market by Japanese corporations. Their participations are still miniscule, but doubled as a percentage of the market in each of 1987 and 1988 with the help of encouragement and guidance by the Ministry of Finance. They are also active in securing positions for their parent companies as lead managers and co-managers of the ever-growing volume of issues by Japanese corporations and government institutions in the international capital markets.

Many of the foreign securities companies maintain research departments and are active in dealing for for foreign and, increasingly, Japanese investors in Japanese equities and bonds. Most of the British houses offer dealing services in UK equities and bonds, and other international securities. This business continues to be disappointing, as the contrast in performance between London and Tokyo Stock Exchanges becomes ever more striking and Japanese investors continue to worry about the risk of further appreciation of the yen against other major international currencies, including sterling. Compared with the difficulties in building a profitable business in their own countries' securities, the foreign securities companies have been relatively quite successful in the business of selling Japanese securities to Japanese investors. This is often attributed to the growing Japanese interest in western analytical research techniques, although it must be admitted that this interest is to date largely an academic one. Nevertheless, the existence of a research department producing high-quality research is a powerful marketing tool. The 22 foreign members of the Tokyo Stock Exchange account only for around 3 percent of market turnover, but this is yielding significant and rising commission revenues.

Foreign securities companies are also becoming more involved in assisting foreign companies raise finance in the Japanese market, listing their shares on the Tokyo Stock Exchange and developing Japanese market strategies. A significant part of the privatisation equity of British Telecom, British Gas and BP was sold in Japan by public offering, and in the latter two cases British houses joined the Japanese management group. Recently many foreign securities companies have started to develop their capacity to assist both Japanese and non-Japanese companies in Mergers and Acquisitions. Japanese companies are increasingly prepared to use M&A as a means of developing overseas markets more rapidly than the traditional 'green field site' method allows.

Most of the overseas acquisitions by Japanese companies have been in the United States, but developments in Europe are encouraging many Japanese companies to look more closely at that continent, both because of the enhanced opportunities that the single market is expected to provide and also because of a fear of being excluded from a 'Fortress Europe'.

Japan is the largest source of investment capital in the world, and foreign securities companies in Japan also play a role in the direction and application of funds to overseas investment projects. Private placements with the major Japanese insurance companies and leasing companies for European or American borrowers are growing in number and size. Japanese investment in overseas property, already a well-known phenomenon in North America, has increased to include Europe, especially the United Kingdom. UK merchant banks have also placed specialist funds such as property funds and leveraged buy-out (LBO) funds with Japanese investors.

The original investment advisory functions of the old representative offices are now carried out by separate investment management companies established under the Investment Advisory Law of 1986. There are two types of licence issued under this law: one permitting the holder to provide investment advice for a fee and the other permitting the provision of full discretionary investment management services. Several of the UK merchant banks have established companies holding both licences and the investment management business is believed to have great potential for UK merchant banking groups whose long experience in international portfolio investment should give them a significant advantage over domestic Japanese competitors. Opportunities will also increase as a result of the decision of the Ministry of Finance gradually to deregulate the rapidly growing pension fund business. Only trust banks and life insurance companies are currently allowed to manage pension funds in Japan.

The maintenance of a significant number of expatriate officers in Japan is also extremely expensive. Nevertheless, operating revenues are increasing steadily and the head offices in London of many UK merchant banks earn very significant revenues as a result of the existence of their Tokyo branches and liaison services performed by them. As the Japanese economy continues to grow and Tokyo becomes ever more important as a financial centre, no merchant bank with international aspirations will be able to ignore Tokyo, and those which are successful in remaining or becoming important international players will not be able to avoid maintaining a significant presence in Japan.

19

❧

THE USA

RAY MINELLA

When Americans use the term 'merchant banking', they are talking about a phenomenon that has no direct counterpart in the United Kingdom. The quick definition is simple: British merchant banking is, in the United States, referred to as *investment banking*; American merchant banking is a specialised part of investment banking. A fuller explanation of US merchant banking requires some background about the evolution of US corporations and the investment bankers who serve them.

From the end of World War II up to the 1960s, American economic might dominated the world. US businesses faced little or no competition from European and Japanese firms. Compared with today, it was a sleepy era. The Federal Reserve discount rate changed only twice during the 1960s. Inflation ran at 6 percent in 1971, which seemed dismayingly high at the time.

The first transition to today's more complicated ways came in the early 1970s, with the first of the OPEC oil shocks. Oil price rises drove increased inflation throughout the 1970s. Decades-old assumptions about interest rates and fixed-income investments became obsolete. The beginnings of competition from Europe and Japan also began to be felt at this time.

The world was changing and few leaders in America's corporations noticed. The 'mandarins', as John Kenneth Galbraith called the managers in charge of America's corporations, ignored their primary obligation, which was to build value for the shareholders who own their companies. Instead, they focused on building sales and size. Competitors from abroad, particularly the Japanese *zaibatsu* firms in cars and electronics, routed long-established US corporations from their dominance of American markets. Corporate America also embarked on a prolonged spate of conglomeratisation, acquiring additional lines of business for the sake of diversification. These businesses generally received insufficient management attention and underperformed their potential. After decades of misaligned priorities, a great deal of wealth was waiting to be tapped.

Investment bankers were in a bind of their own. In May 1975, fixed commissions on securities trading were abolished in the United States, a step that eroded profitability. A similar move took place in 1978, with the advent of

'415 shelf registration': instead of calling on their investment banker to assemble a syndicate, firms could now simply notify the Securities and Exchange Commission (SEC) of their intent to issue a security, and then invite Wall Street firms to bid on it. Traditional activities were changing from relationship-based time-consuming transactions into commodity-like services. Competition on price was the crucial consideration.

Thus Wall Street investment banks needed a new source of business to offset dwindling profitability, while more entrepreneurial business people looked to unlock slumbering corporate wealth. These two needs meshed exactly, although awareness of this unity of interest was slow in developing.

At first, this led to a new emphasis on mergers and acquisitions: investment banks were drawn to the fee-based income, which was not dependent on market volume. Corporations needed a way to maximise shareholder value, and M&A offered a ready method.

Another trend in favour of M&A and the creation of wealth came with a change in the way accounting was viewed. Investment bankers and their corporate clients began to carry their analysis of business possibilities beyond generally accepted accounting practices and to look on today's value as the *present value of tomorrow's cash flows.*

This was a major change from the traditional spirit of accounting, which records an asset at historical cost and depreciates it over its useful life, and measures profitability through the calculation of net income. Investment bankers observed that these criteria often obscured rather than illuminated a corporation's true value. The rapid inflation of the 1970s resulted in an asset's replacement or market-value being significantly in excess of the value stated on the corporation's balance sheet. The net income accounting requirements imposed by regulatory authorities meant that cash flow was a much more dependable measure of a company's health. 'Net income' includes a number of non-cash-related expenses, and so bankers and their clients took it upon themselves to recast traditional financial statements to determine the exact amount of cash generated by the company's operations.

Yet another trend that gave impetus to M&A was the emergence of a new breed of entrepreneur – the owner–manager. This new kind of business executive was impatient with companies that underperformed due to a focus on sales and size rather than cash flow. In the words of one well-known owner–manager, 'knowing that your financial compensation is directly tied to the operating performance of your company concentrates the mind wonderfully'.

The debt side proved to be the most significant and innovative area for financing large, wealth-creating transactions. The crucial instrument turned out to be junk bonds. At first glance, they were not an obvious choice. The junk bond scene in the late 1970s was small, comprised mostly of the instruments of firms that were once rated investment-grade, but had fallen on hard times (known as 'fallen angels'). Investors approached junk as a speculative equity play: I'll buy the junk debt of XYZ corporation for 10 cents on the dollar, say, and if I'm lucky it will eventually be worth par. Gradually and tentatively, a few investment banks arranged junk new issues for small, new firms unable to issue investment grade debt.

Mike Milken of Drexel Burnham Lambert deserves the credit for recognising the extraordinary potential of junk bonds. He saw that relatively few issuers of new junk bonds ever defaulted. In the second stage of this market's development, Milken and Drexel assiduously promoted junk bonds to middle-tier industrial firms as a way of financing growth cheaply and easily.

For issuers, junk bonds offered some very appealing advantages. Unlike bank financing, junk bonds were a flexible and abundant source of financing. Unlike private placements with insurance companies (the only other major source of non-equity financing until the early 1980s for small growth-oriented firms), the covenants were simple. If the firm grew fast enough, future cash flow would pay off the debt easily. Junk bonds also proved to be an effective substitute to proprietary managements for equity financing, since the tax system in the United States favoured debt and firms could access the capital they needed without surrendering equity control.

But issuers alone would not have sufficed, and part of Milken's innovation was to help create an active secondary market for junk bonds by not only underwriting securities, but creating pools of capital to buy them. Often, a Drexel junk bond issuer, at Milken's recommendation, would raise excess proceeds in an offering which would then be available to invest in junk bonds issued by another Drexel client. As a result, Drexel clients might be issuers one day and investors the next. The relationship between issuers and investors was self-renewing and symbiotic.

Eventually this secondary market acquired more breadth and depth, attracting mutual funds and institutional money-managers, insurance companies, and savings and loan institutions. For these investors, junk offered high yields with comparative safety. The existence of a liquid secondary market, even in the nascent form of the early 1980s, changed the investment time horizon of junk bonds and mezzanine securities. No longer was it necessary to assume an investment had to be held to maturity. This changed the risk profile of the investment, and helped to create the attractive public market for LBO paper that characterised the history to the late 1980s.

Another appeal to investors stems from the peculiar hybrid nature of junk bonds. At least in theory, junk securities are riskier than investment grade securities, but they are not quite as risky as equities. Junk bonds have some equity traits, since to judge them accurately one must pay close attention to asset appreciation. Moreover, the movements of interest rates usually do not affect junk bonds the way they affect most other kinds of debt. Equity, junk and investment grade – each of these types of security has a different level of volatility, which rarely move in unison. This creates diversification possibilities, which are always attractive to investors.

In the third stage of junk bonds, once these growth companies were comfortable with junk financing, some Drexel clients began pursuing mergers and acquisitions. Drexel played a major role in creating the entrepreneurial class of corporate raiders and was prominently involved in many of the highly visible takeovers of the early and mid 1980s. A raider would line up bank financing and perhaps an equity participant to do a financing, and then Drexel would issue their well-known 'highly confident' letter, in which they stated they were highly confident they could place the subordinated debt associated with this transaction. The 'highly confident' letter made acquisitions viable that would have been unthinkable in the past.

In 1985, Drexel had almost 50 percent of the market in junk bonds and was making lots of money. At best, Drexel's competitors could hope only to match the junk bond leader's performance for a high yield client – they could not surpass it.

Merrill Lynch devised the strategy of using a large bridge loan to create opportunity. Instead of handing the client a 'highly confident' letter, Merrill committed the firm to handing the client a cheque. Some critics scoffed at bridge loans – or 'mezzanine financing' – as a way for laggards to buy their way into the junk bond business, ignoring the fundamental reality of this kind of transaction. Instead, mezzanine financing was a different way of approaching mergers and acquisitions, in which the timely availability of capital often makes the difference between success and failure. To put it simply, merchant banking provides large-scale short-term financing for M&A transactions.

How does a transaction work? It involves integrating all the disciplines necessary to analyse value, as well as initiate, design, sell and trade securities. If the XYZ corporation wants to undertake a leveraged buyout, it will approach its bank, which will assemble an equity participant, a senior debt participant (that is, bank loans), and the subordinated debt component.

The equity participant is likely to be one of the large LBO funds such as Kohlberg Kravis Roberts, or Forstmann Little (or, perhaps, the investment banking firm itself). These are large pools of money, put up mostly by large institutional investors, to take positions in these high-risk, high-return situations. The LBO firms appeared in the mid 1970s. Kohlberg Kravis Roberts pioneered this manoeuvre in which a pool of money is assembled to buy the assets that firms spun off, or to buy the entire firm. The initial investments these LBO funds undertook were small, and they were seen at first as narrow speciality. But with the advent of merchant banking, they became the primary vehicle for taking a large equity position in leveraged transactions.

Merchant bankers in America are intimately tied with all other phases of investment banking, since any given transaction may enlist the talents of everyone. Deals are often very complicated, involving private placements, new issues, divestitures, recapitalisations and a variety of other activities.

The evolution of merchant banking has been turbulent, but it has followed readily identified stages.

1. First came Drexel's 'highly confident' letter, which was not a legally binding commitment. But since the firm's credibility as an investment banker hinged on the reputation of its letters, if a tranche of subordinated debt to finance a transaction was not selling, Drexel could (and perhaps sometimes did) step in and buy part of the debt issue, in effect becoming a participant.
2. Bridge loans were the next stage. After the firm provided a bridge loan, it would then help issue the subordinated debt necessary to pay off the loan. This sped the process of securing financing in a business where speed is all-important.
3. Now firms like Merrill Lynch provide bridge loans, subordinated debt *and* buy part of the equity. The theory is that if we have done our homework properly and identified this as a fine investment, we should not hesitate to take a significant minority position. After all, the rate of return for equity is typically much more attractive than for senior debt or subordinated debt (which includes junk bonds). The exact vehicle for taking this minority stake varies: sometimes it is a special LBO fund, sometimes it is the investment bank's holding company, and often a combination of the two.

Investment banks will probably move toward yet another stage, and keep larger portions of the equity for themselves, assuming a majority stake and perhaps even managerial control. Indeed most major investment banks, one way or another, already have such funds in place.

US merchant bankers must pay careful attention to conflicts of interest, which can crop up at all stages of a transaction. A proposed hostile target may be a client, and a merchant banker will be obliged to turn down the deal; or different sub-groups of the same organisation may find themselves competing for business. This complex subject lies beyond the scope of this chapter, but vetting transactions for conflicts is done at the highest levels of investment banking firms.

The transition for investment banks has been from acting solely as an agent, to acting as a principal for debt securities, then as a principal for equity securities. In a way, this trend was a throwback to the earliest days of 'merchant banking', in which houses would act not merely as intermediaries, but take a position in a transaction as a participant, using their own capital. Then as now, merchant banking is using one's own capital to create an opportunity for oneself and one's clients. The term has not quite come full circle, since investment bankers generally do not sit on the boards of publicly held corporations, but the crisp distinction between principal, agent and client grows blurrier with each passing day.

20

❧

THE MIDDLE EAST

CHRISTOPHER ARNANDER

The Middle East, in its financial context, is not a precise geographical term, but is regarded as consisting of the countries of the Arabian peninsula, together with, at various times, Egypt, Jordan, Lebanon, Syria, Iraq and Iran. When the price of oil rose in 1973 and the following years, large surpluses accrued to the area's oil producing countries. These surpluses have been employed in internal development, in foreign policy initiatives and in various kinds of aid to the Third World. A large amount of the surpluses belonging to the public and private sector of several of the countries – notably Saudi Arabia, Kuwait, Qatar, United Arab Emirates, Oman and Bahrain – have been recycled into banking, securities and real estate markets around the world. The growth in these funds in the 1970s and 1980s created significant opportunities for international financial institutions offering investment, securities, capital markets, banking and general advisory services.
Table 20.1 gives details of the largest Arab-controlled banks.

Table 20.1. Largest Arab-controlled banks

Bank and head office	Total assets* ($billion)	World rank†
Rafidan Bank, Baghdad	46.0	85
BCCI Holdings, Luxembourg	19.6	204
National Commercial Bank, Jeddah	18.9	211
Arab Banking Corporation, Bahrain	17.5	203
Al Ubaf Banking Group, Paris	14.4	238
Arab Bank, Amman	13.5	244
Banque Nationale d'Algérie, Algiers	12.3	259
Commercial Bank of Syria, Damascus	11.8	275
Banque Extérieure d'Algérie, Algiers	11.4	279
National Bank of Kuwait, Kuwait	11.2	284
First American Bankshares, Washington	9.6	315
Gulf International Bank, Bahrain	8.9	337
Riyad Bank, Riyadh	8.9	339
Crédit Populaire d'Algérie, Algiers	8.5	352
National Bank of Egypt, Cairo	7.4	504

Table taken from *The Banker*, July 1988† and December 1988*.

Institutional structure

The institutional structure of the financial community varies from country to country, but the following types of organisations are to be found throughout the region:

- Government financial agencies
- Commercial banks
- Investment companies and investment banks
- Multilateral organisations
- Aid and development organisations

These organisations have played a role in recycling surpluses, both within the respective economies and in external markets.

Government agencies

These consist of central banks, monetary authorities and other government financial agencies. Central banks and monetary authorities fulfil, in the Middle East countries, their classic roles of controlling the banks and the money supply, acting as lender of last resort, issuing the currency and managing the reserves; they generally oversee the financial system in each country. In addition, in order to deploy excess revenues and to provide social security for their citizens, long-term investing institutions have been set up by several governments. These entities are growing at a rapid rate, as they collect contributions, based on monthly salaries, which are funded by both employees and employers, on behalf of populations which are still comparatively young. Owing to shortage of suitable local investments and to find profitable investment outlets, these organisations have also been active investors in overseas markets. They fulfil many of the functions carried out by pension funds and life insurance companies in the economies of the Western Europe, the Far East and North America. Consequently, the growth of life insurance companies in the area has not been very significant. Indeed, there are some countries in which life insurance companies are not allowed to operate at all, although composite insurance is well established through locally owned companies, joint ventures and insurance broking agencies. The growth of the oil industry and the industrialisation of the area have created significant openings for the London and other international insurance markets, in conjunction with Middle East insurance interests.

Commercial banks

In some countries the banking system is indigenously owned, such as Kuwait; in others, there is foreign participation, ranging from minority interests in locally incorporated banks (Saudi Arabia) to limited branching rights for foreign banks (Bahrain, Oman and United Arab Emirates). In nearly all the countries, the government has had, and often still has, a stake in certain of the private sector banks. In Saudi Arabia and Kuwait, government participation has been designed to support banks in the private sector. In Egypt, Syria and Iraq, the banks are government-owned as a result of the political philosophy or history of those countries.

Investment companies and investment banks

To recycle the surpluses of the region, a number of investment companies and investment banks have been formed. Although their activities are somewhat different from typical Western investment banks, they have demonstrated an entrepreneurial approach to overseas investment and have had a number of successes in the capital markets.

This type of institution came to prominence in the early 1970s in Kuwait through three strongly capitalised investment companies, often known in the international capital markets as 'the three Ks': Kuwait Investment Company, Kuwait Foreign Trading, Contracting and Investment Company, and Kuwait International Investment Company. Their formation was followed by the formation of other investment companies in Kuwait and other countries of the Gulf, one of the largest being the Abu Dhabi Investment Company. The Kuwaiti companies became very active in capital matters, pioneering many new issues denominated in Kuwaiti Dinars, organising syndicated loans and managing investment portfolios for clients. A decade later, Arabian Investment Banking Corporation (Investcorp) was formed in Bahrain, with overseas offices. It has been very successful, backed by a wide range of the leading citizens of the Gulf, who participate in some of their transactions: Investcorp has carried out a number of very profitable and high profile transactions, particularly leveraged buy-outs in the United States.

Multilateral organisations

There are a number of intergovernment or official organisations such as the Gulf Co-operation Council (GCC) and the Organisation of Arab Petroleum Exporting Countries (OAPEC), which have given rise to or encouraged the creation of multilateral banks and investment companies. Notable are two large consortium banks, based in Bahrain, namely Arab Banking Corporation and Gulf International Bank. Formed by OAPEC, the Arab Petroleum Investments Corporation (APICORP), based in Dharhan, is active in the development of petroleum-related projects and in financial markets generally. In Kuwait, Gulf Investment Corporation is well established as an investment company, with activities in the Gulf and elsewhere. All these organisations are owned directly or indirectly by Arab governments and contribute significantly to the Middle East financial scene.

Aid and development organisations

One of the ways in which Middle East countries have deployed their assets is through the formation of aid organisations. Modelled on the World Bank, and often co-operating with it, these funds have made a generous contribution to the economies of less developed countries, particularly in the Islamic world, by advising on and providing finance for projects. In addition to the funds of individual countries, a multilateral aid organisation has also been established, the Arab Fund for Economic and Social Development, based in Kuwait. This is a vehicle for co-operation among the Arab countries in providing development finance, mainly in the Arab world.

Industrial companies and stockmarkets

Industrialisation in the Middle East has been hampered by the small local market and by the comparative absence of indigenous labour, but strenuous efforts have been and are being made to build up an industrial structure. Government development funds, concessionary loans, tax holidays, cheap (or free) land and cheap energy are among the weapons used to foster the growth of an industrial base. Refineries, aluminium and petrochemical plants, shipping, construction and construction materials are some of the area of industrialisation, which have created financing opportunities for international investment banks, as well as local banks, which have often co-operated with each other in the raising of funds. Industries are, in some cases, entirely owned by local investors. In the industrial cities of Jubail and Yanbu in Saudi Arabia, huge joint ventures have been created between Saudi investors, such as PETROMIN and Saudi Basic Industries Corporation, and international oil companies in the downstream area of the oil industry. Many of the incentives are designed to attract international companies to form joint ventures with local investors and assist technology transfer.

A number of the new industries and financial institutions have been financed in part by issues of stock on the local stock markets, participation in which is normally restricted to citizens of the area. Development of stockmarkets in the Middle East has suffered from the speculative excesses of the 'Souk Al Manakh' crisis during the early 1980s, which seriously affected many investors in Kuwait and put a damper on the development of stockmarkets in the region. However, there are a few dozen banks and companies in the region which are quoted on their home stock exchange, and attempts are being made to improve systems and liquidity and to increase cross-border stockmarket co-operation, particularly in the GCC countries.

Trading houses

Much of the economic activity of the region has been developed by trading houses which started their business lives as importers, later becoming industrialists and investors. In the second and third generation of some of these trading houses, which are typically organised as private partnerships, controlled by one or more of the founding families, they have come to be organised and managed very effectively along the most modern international lines. A number have become active and successful investors, both in portfolio and in direct investments around the world.

International dimensions

The Middle East financing institutions are well represented outside their own home bases. Some of them, such as the major consortium banks, Arab Banking Corporation and Gulf International Bank, have extensive offices and affiliates overseas, with operations in London, New York and other major centres around the world. Several joint ventures, incorporated in Western countries, have been in existence for 15 years, such as the two major Franco-Arab banking consortia, Union de Banques Arabes et Francaises (UBAF) and Banque Arabe et Internationale d'Investissement (BAII), which bring together French and Arab banks, coupled with banks from other countries. In London, several UK registered consortium banks have been formed, some entirely owned by investors of one country (United Bank of Kuwait) others owned by investors of more than one country (Saudi International Bank, which is 55 percent Saudi owned, with the balance of the capital being owned by a group of major multinational banks). Most of these consortium banks combine investment and commercial banking under one roof, and have appeared in many transactions as partners of Western banks. London is also the base of the Kuwait Investment Office, which has established itself as a large, active and sophisticated investor in the United Kingdom and other markets.

   In addition to the large presence of Arab institutions in the world's leading financial centres, Western banks have participated in the Middle East financial scene through joint ventures, subsidiaries, branches and affiliates. Regional financial centres, such as Beirut in the 1960s and 1970s and Bahrain in the 1970s and 1980s have played host to many international investment and commercial banks striving to participate in the opportunities presented by the Middle East markets. Bahrain has had some success as a regional financial centre, offering the mechanism of offshore banking units (OBUs) which enable major banks to operate throughout the region (though restricted within Bahrain) and the ability for investment houses to establish representative offices covering the neighbouring countries.

Islamic finance

No description of financing in the Middle East would be complete without some reference to financial and banking services provided in accordance with the Shariah, or Islamic principles. In Islam, as in Christianity, there is abhorrence of usury. Although there are many interpretations as to what is appropriate, the essence of Islamic finance involves the provision of non-interest-bearing capital. There are several recognised formulae, the most common of which are:

1. *Mudarabah* Trust financing, under which a trustee manages the owner's capital, in return for a share of the profits, with losses falling exclusively on the owner.
2. *Musharakah* Participation financing, under which funds are provided by several parties in the form of equity, profits and losses being shared proportionately to the contribution of each party.
3. *Murabahah* Cost-plus financing, under which materials or goods are acquired on behalf of a user and sold to him at a later date for cost, plus an agreed mark-up.
4. *Ijara* Leasing, renting or hiring agreements.

In most cases, there is an implied rate of interest or an assured rate of return, so that the transactions are more like fixed interest than equity investments. Instruments such as zero coupon bonds are accepted by some investors, even though the discount approximates interest by another name. Government bonds are considered acceptable by others, because the interest is not payable by individuals, but by governments which are, by definition, more powerful than, and cannot be exploited by, individual investors. Some accept forward foreign exchange and futures transactions. Most accept sale-and-guaranteed-repurchase of commodities (Murabahah) and leasing (Ijara).

In the Middle East countries, Islamic instruments and institutions have been created within a non-Islamic banking environment, while in Pakistan the entire banking system has been changed. At least three categories of institution are involved in the market:

1. Overtly Islamic institutions, such as the Islamic Development Bank, the Kuwait Finance House, the Dubai Islamic Bank, the Al Baraka group, Dar Al Maal. In 1988, this group was joined by the newly incorporated Alrajhi Banking and Investment Corporation, Riyadh, whose shares were offered successfully in 1988 to the Saudi investing public. The new Alrajhi offers financial and banking services, on Islamic lines, through a network of branches throughout Saudi Arabia and an affiliate in London, all inherited from its predecessor firm. It offers strong competition for the Saudi commercial banks.
2. Banks in Islamic countries, offering Islamic products alongside normal bank products, and Western banks and investment companies controlled by Islamic investors.
3. Western banks offering Islamic products, such as specialised unit trusts,

run in accordance with Islamic principles, and financings of the type described above.

The Islamic Development Bank, Jeddah, funded by forty-two Islamic countries, was established in 1975 and occupies a central role in the world of Islamic finance. It fosters the economic development and social progress of member countries and Muslim communities, in accordance with the principles of the Shariah. In Saudi Arabia, the Shariah prevails, with the result that interest on loans cannot be enforced in the courts. This has given rise to difficulties for Saudi banks and for foreign banks extending facilities in the Kingdom, which have been unable to collect on their loans. However, the problem has been greatly mitigated by the work of the Banking Disputes Committee which was set up in 1987 and which has been effective in resolving disputes between banks and their customers.

There is a considerable volume of literature on the subject of Islamic banking and finance, backed by a large number of conferences and discussions. The subject is an extremely live one in the Islamic countries, particularly at a time when there is a world-wide movement towards the strengthening of traditional Islamic values. Generally, despite poor results from some Islamic institutions, the Islamic banking and finance movement flourished in the late 1980s and there is every expectation that it can be expected to gather strength in the years to come.

POSTSCRIPT

WILLIAM KAY

While students, practitioners and commentators will continue to argue over the use of the term 'merchant banking', no one doubts that the function of merchant banks, as practised in the City of London in various forms for centuries past, will continue into the twenty-first century and beyond. Corporate clients will still need financially-orientated strategic and tactical advice, and the assistance of experts who can execute the appropriate transactions resulting from that advice. Clients big and small will continue to require investment management services of varying complexity and sophistication to ensure that their surplus funds are deployed to the best effect.

What has changed dramatically in the past decade, and is likely to go on changing rapidly for several decades to come, is the environment in which those services are performed. Customers are, simply, becoming better educated at all levels and higher standards of living are giving them greater opportunities to exploit and resources to be deployed. The mystique in which the City was once cloaked is being drawn to one side, and that can be only healthy for all concerned. An educated audience may be more demanding, but it will also be less frightened to listen to more innovative suggestions.

The financial services industry has responded to these developments by itself becoming more competitive. Its stock-in-trade always was ideas and their presentation, and it is now able to give full rein to the most imaginative ways of developing both aspects of their offerings.

However, while greater competition is generally welcomed, it is ever liable to produce excesses which raise doubts about the future development of the industry. In the case of merchant banks, two prime concerns have been the greater emphasis on short-term performance stimuli and on the priority accorded to individual transactions as opposed to long-term relationships.

But it should be borne in mind that such an innovative and entrepreneurial activity as merchant banking, populated with highly intelligent, energetic and articulate operators, can do no other than push at the boundaries of acceptable practice. They would hardly be doing their job were they not to test the limits of their art, for art it is. Those ideas which do not find favour with customers will be discarded, either on the spot or gradually as customer preferences become clear.

For it is a fact that banking clients do not always know what they want from their financial servants. Preservation or enhancement of capital, certainly – but at no danger to reputation and the smallest practicable exposure to risk and therefore uncertainty. These conflicting requirements cannot always be satisfactorily reconciled, and the search for the ideal balance of advantage is endless.

These demands would be challenging enough if merchant banking were confined to the British Isles. But it never was, and two of the most important developments of the late twentieth century have been greater freedom of international trade and the technological advances in communications to enable traders and investors to exploit the new freedoms.

Marshall McLuhan's global village is growing closer all the time, and one of the main topics of conversation in the public bar and across the garden fence has been the business of business. Money puts a precise value on communications, for it is possible to judge whether the profit exceeds the expense. So it was only to be expected that financial markets would be the first to make use successively of telegraph, telephone, telex, television and computerisation.

This meant simultaneously that overseas organisations offering the equivalent of merchant banking services could easily invade the British market once regulations permitted, and British merchant banks had to establish outposts around the world to provide the new standard of international service which rapidly became the norm.

International expansion will be a dominant theme of the years to come as more barriers are lifted and more countries are able to avail themselves of more sophisticated financial services. The move towards a single internal European market, targeted on 1992, will see the next great explosion in cross-border activity as the inhibitions traditionally associated with national borders are removed. The Pacific Rim has long been identified as another huge area on the verge of tremendous growth, between its local countries and with the rest of the world. And, further ahead, South America and Africa beckon.

These represent a formidable catalogue of opportunities for merchant banks, in whatever form they present themselves, and those who work in them. The relaxed, even mannered, style of earlier times may be gone for ever, but the essential challenge remains: to provide clients with financial services of value.

APPENDIX A

❦

BRITISH MERCHANT BANKING AND SECURITIES HOUSES ASSOCIATION

Members

As at 30 November 1989

ALLIED PROVINCIAL SECURITIES PLC
  155 St Vincent Street, Glasgow G2 5NN (041-204 1885)

HENRY ANSBACHER & CO. LIMITED
  One Mitre Square, EC3A 5AN (01-283 2500)

ARBUTHNOT LATHAM BANK LIMITED
  131 Finsbury Pavement, Moorgate, EC2A 1AY (01-628 9876)

BANK JULIUS BAER & CO. LTD
  Bevis Marks House, Bevis Marks, EC3A 7NE (01-623 4211)

BARCLAYS DE ZOETE WEDD HOLDINGS LIMITED
  Ebbgate House, 2 Swan Lane, EC4R 3TS (01-623 2323)

BARINGS PLC
  8 Bishopsgate, EC2N 4AE (01-283 8833)

BRITISH & COMMONWEALTH MERCHANT BANK PLC
  66 Cannon Street, EC4N 6AE (01-248 0900)

THE BRITISH LINEN BANK LIMITED
  PO Box 49, 4 Melville Street, Edinburgh, EH3 7NS (031-453 1919)

BROWN SHIPLEY HOLDINGS PLC
  Founders Court, Lothbury, EC2R 7HE (01-606 9833)

JAMES CAPEL & CO
  James Capel House, PO Box 551, 6 Bevis Marks, EC3A 7JQ (01-621 0011)

CAZENOVE & CO
  12 Tokenhouse Yard, EC2R 7AN (01-588 2828)

CHARTERHOUSE PLC
  1 Paternoster Row, St Paul's, EC4M 7DH (01-248 4000)

CLOSE BROTHERS LIMITED
  36 Great St Helen's, EC3A 6AP (01-283 2241)

CREDIT LYONNAIS CAPITAL MARKETS LTD
  Broadwalk House, 5 Appold Street, EC2A 2DA (01-588 4000)

CREDIT SUISSE FIRST BOSTON LTD
  2A Great Titchfield Street, W1P 7AA (01-322 4000)

DAIWA EUROPE LIMITED
PO Box 72, 5 King William Street, EC4N 7AX (01-548 8080)

DAWNAY, DAY & CO. LIMITED
15 Grosvenor Gardens, SW1W 0BD (01-834 8060)

DEUTSCHE BANK CAPITAL MARKETS LIMITED
150 Leadenhall Street, EC3V 4RJ (01-971 7000)

DREXEL BURNHAM LAMBERT SECURITIES LTD
Drexel Burnham House, 1 Alie Street, E1 8DB (01-325 9797)

ENSKILDA SECURITIES
26 Finsbury Square, EC2A 1DS (01-638 3500)

ROBERT FLEMING HOLDINGS LIMITED
25 Copthall Avenue, EC2R 7DR (01-638 5858)

GOLDMAN SACHS INTERNATIONAL LTD
8/10 New Fetter Lane, EC4A 1DB (01-489 2000)

GRANVILLE & CO. LIMITED
Mint House, 77 Mansell Street, E1 8AF (01-488 1212)

GRESHAM TRUST PLC
Barrington House, Gresham Street, EC2V 7HE (01-606 6474)

GUINNESS MAHON & CO. LIMITED
32 St Mary at Hill, EC3P 3AJ (01-623 9333)

HAMBROS BANK LIMITED
41 Tower Hill, EC3N 4HA (01-480 5000)

HILL SAMUEL BANK LIMITED
PO Box 20, 100 Wood Street, EC2P 2AJ (01-628 8011)

HOARE GOVETT LIMITED
4 Broadgate, EC2M 7LE (01-601 0101)

LEOPOLD JOSEPH & SONS LIMITED
31/45 Gresham Street, EC2V 7EA (01-588 2323)

KLEINWORT BENSON GROUP PLC
PO Box 560, 20 Fenchurch Street, EC3P 3DB (01-623 8000)

LAZARD BROTHERS & CO. LIMITED
PO Box 516, 21 Moorfields, EC2P 2HT (01-588 2721)

LLOYDS MERCHANT BANK LIMITED
40–46 Queen Victoria Street, EC4P 4EL (01-248 2244)

LONDON ITALIAN BANK LIMITED
20 Cannon Street, EC4M 6XD (01-236 7464)

MANUFACTURERS HANOVER LIMITED
1–11 John Adam Street, WC2N 6HT (01-932 4000)

MERRILL LYNCH INTERNATIONAL & CO
Ropemaker Place, 25 Ropemaker Street, EC2Y 9LY (01-628 1000)

SAMUEL MONTAGU & CO. LIMITED
10 Lower Thames Street, EC3R 6AE (01-260 9000)

MORGAN GRENFELL GROUP PLC
PO Box 56, 23 Great Winchester Street, EC2P 2AX (01-588 4545)

J P MORGAN SECURITIES LTD.
PO Box 124, 30 Throgmorton Street, EC2N 2NT (01-600 7545)

MORGAN STANLEY INTERNATIONAL
Kingsley House, 1A Wimpole Street, W1M 7AA (01-709 3000)

NATWEST INVESTMENT BANK LIMITED
Drapers Gardens, 12 Throgmorton Avenue, EC2P 2ES (01-382 1000)

NEVILLE INDUSTRIAL SECURITIES LIMITED
Neville House, 42–46 Hagley Road, Birmingham B16 8PZ (021-454 5431)

THE NIKKO SECURITIES CO (EUROPE) LIMITED
55 Victoria Street, SW1H 0EU (01-799 2222)

NIPPON KANGYO KAKUMARU (EUROPE) LIMITED
18 Finsbury Circus, EC2M 7AT (01-638 4871)

NOMURA INTERNATIONAL PLC
24 Monument Street, EC3R 8AJ (01-283 8811)

PARIBAS LIMITED
33 Wigmore Street, W1H 0BN (01-355 2000)

PK ENGLISH TRUST COMPANY LIMITED
Carthusian Court, 12 Carthusian Street, EC1M 6EB (01-796 1200)

PRUDENTIAL–BACHE SECURITIES (UK) INC
9 Devonshire Square, EC2M 4HP (01-548 4000)

REA BROTHERS LIMITED
Alderman's House, Alderman's Walk, EC2M 3XR (01-623 1155)

RIGGS A P BANK LTD
21 Great Winchester Street, EC2N 2HH (01-588 7575)

N M ROTHSCHILD & SONS LIMITED
PO Box 185, New Court, St Swithin's Lane, EC4P 4DU (01-280 5000)

SALOMON BROTHERS INTERNATIONAL LIMITED
Victoria Plaza, 111 Buckingham Palace Road, SW1W 0SB (01-721 2000)

SANWA INTERNATIONAL LIMITED
PO Box 245, 1 Undershaft, EC3A 8BR (01-623 7991)

SAUDI INTERNATIONAL BANK
99 Bishopsgate, EC2M 3TB (01-638 2323)

SCANDINAVIAN BANK GROUP PLC
2–6 Cannon Street, EC4M 6XX (01-236 6090)

J. HENRY SCHRODER WAGG & CO. LIMITED
120 Cheapside, EC2V 6DS (01-382 6000)

SHEARSON LEHMAN HUTTON HOLDINGS PLC
One Broadgate, EC2M 7HA (01-601 0011)

SINGER & FRIEDLANDER HOLDINGS LIMITED
21 New Street, Bishopsgate, EC2M 4HR (01-623 3000)

SMITH & WILLIAMSON SECURITIES
No 1 Riding House Street, W1A 3AS (01-637 5377)

SMITH NEW COURT PLC
PO Box 293, 24 St Swithin's Lane, EC4N 8AE (01-626 1544)

STANDARD CHARTERED MERCHANT BANK LIMITED
33–36 Gracechurch Street, EC3V 0AX (01-623 8711).

3i CORPORATE FINANCE LTD
91 Waterloo Road, SE1 8XP (01-928 7822)

UBS/PHILLIPS & DREW SECURITIES LTD
100 Liverpool Street, EC2M 2RH (01-901 3333)

WALLACE, SMITH TRUST CO LIMITED
77 London Wall, EC2N 1AB (01-638 6444)

S G WARBURG GROUP PLC
1 Finsbury Avenue, EC2M 2PA (01-606 1066)

YAMAICHI INTERNATIONAL (EUROPE) LIMITED
111–117 Finsbury Pavement, EC2A 1EQ (01-638 5599)

INDEX